Duncan J. D. Smith

ONLY IN
MARSEILLE

A Guide to Unique Locations,
Hidden Corners and Unusual Objects

Photographs by
Duncan J. D. Smith
except where stated otherwise

The Urban Explorer

Sailors' ex-votos hanging in the Basilica of Notre-Dame de la Garde (see no. 38)

Contents

Introduction

> "Marseille, white, fervid, full of life and energy…
> the younger sister of Tyre and Carthage, the successor of them
> in the empire of the Mediterranean…old, yet always young."
>
> Alexandre Dumas, *The Count of Monte Cristo,* 1844–1846

The words of French author Alexandre Dumas (1802–1870) date back several centuries but still ring true. Marseille, the oldest and second largest city in France, remains quintessentially a Mediterranean port. It is also still as much a place of the future as it is of the past.

Located near the mouth of the River Rhône, Marseille is ringed by limestone hills. Its seaside setting is as alluring as that of Nice, with the added attraction of offshore islands and a series of rocky coves *(calanques)*, one of which provides the city with its Old Port (Vieux Port).

The story of Marseille stretches back over two millennia. Legend asserts that a Greek mariner from Asia Minor, Protis, made landfall here and fell in love with a local princess, Gyptis. Together they founded Massalia, a Hellenised city-state trading in wine and slaves. Historians tell us that the mariner represents Ionian Greek colonists from Phocaea in what is now Turkey, who founded Massalia around 600 BC to establish trade links with the Gauls; the princess represents the Segobriges, an Iron Age Celto-Ligurian tribe already present in the region. The name Massalia, whence Marseille derives, means "(city) at the end of the sea".

In 49 BC, Massalia lost its extramural assets to the Roman Republic but retained its autonomy as a maritime trading concern, as it did after its capture by the Visigoths in the 5th century AD. Even during the 10th century, when it became part of the region of Provence, it kept its frontier spirit. Only in 1252 did Charles of Anjou (1226–1285) bring it forcibly under French suzerainty, and not until 1486 did it join the Kingdom of France.

Over the next four centuries, Marseille grew to become the country's commercial and colonial gateway, drawing merchants, migrants, labourers, and exiles from Europe, Africa, and Asia. Its national importance was acknowledged during the French Revolution, when anti-royalists marched to Paris singing *La Marseillaise*, the First Republic's national anthem.

Although 19th century industrialisation benefited home-grown products such as soap, candles, *pastis*, and even playing cards, Marseille was first and foremost a colonial *entrepôt* handling and processing goods from its client ports. By 1840 it was the fifth largest port in the world and within a century over 60% of its exports were processed colonial goods. Recession of sea traffic during the mid-20th century, worsened by German Occupation during the Second World War, therefore hit hard. Thereafter, unemployment, organised crime, and social divisions exacerbated by an influx of decolonised immigrants saw Marseille's reputation manifested as the 'Wicked City'. Despite this, the Marseillaise remained self-assured and by the turn of the 21st century their city was again on the up. Declared Europe's most cosmopolitan city, the place once seen by travellers as little more than a springboard for Provence, is fast becoming a diverse visitor destination in its own right.

Only in Marseille is for independent cultural travellers wishing to get beneath the city's skin. This is the Marseille of Celtic ruins and modern museums, colonial ghosts and ethnic enclaves, street art and culinary delights. The fifty-five locations represent the author's odyssey through the city, showcasing its famous and less well-known sights. Marseille boasts a bewildering 111 official neighbourhoods *(quartiers)* named after former villages. Fortunately, they are grouped into sixteen boroughs *(arrondissements)*, which themselves are organised into eight sectors *(secteurs)*.

Secteur I (1st and 7th Arrondissements) encompasses much of the Old Port (Vieux Port), as well as the Frioul Archipelago (Îles du Frioul). Highlights include an Art Deco opera house, the Abbey of Saint Victor, and the Château d'If. Immediately north is Secteur II (2nd and 3rd Arrondissements), including Le Panier, the site of the ancient Greek colony, as well as the Euroméditerranée Zone cultural quarter. Secteur III to the east (4th and 5th Arrondissements) contains the Palais Longchamps and the city's old astronomical observatory.

Secteur IV covers part of the southern suburbs (6th and 8th Arrondissements), including the iconic Basilica of Notre-Dame de la Garde and the Vélodrome Stadium. The rest of the southern suburbs are covered by Secteur V (9th and 10th Arrondissements), wherein lie country homes *(bastides)* and the best of the rugged coastline.

Secteur VI (11th and 12th Arrondissements) covers the eastern suburbs, with their contrasting attractions of a pre-Roman citadel and a shrine to cinema. The northern suburbs are also split across two sectors: Secteur VII (13th and 14th Arrondissements), with its soap factory and Armenian connections, and Secteur VIII (15th and 16th Arrondissements), including Buddhist pagodas and the artists' village of L'Estaque.

Walking is the best way to get around the city, with a network of buses and trams for the suburbs and beyond. So, whether swimming through an underwater museum, exploring a unique seaside garden, trying your hand at *pétanque*, or shopping in a shipping container, *Only in Marseille* will encourage readers to embark on their own urban expedition.

Duncan J. D. Smith, Marseille & Vienna

1 The Remains of Ancient Massalia

Secteur I (1st Arrondissement), the Jardin des Vestiges and Marseille History Museum (Musée d'Histoire de Marseille) at 2 Rue Henri Barbusse

Humans have lived in the Marseille area for at least 36,000 years. The archaeological evidence includes Palaeolithic wall art in the Cosquer Cave (34,000 BC) and Neolithic brick dwellings near the railway station (6000 BC) (see no. 23). Evidence pertaining to the Iron Age Celto-Ligurian people, the Segobriges, who held sway during the early-1st millennium BC, is in the form of hilltop citadels (see no. 47). The most tangible evidence from antiquity, however, dates from 600 BC and later, when Ionian Greek colonists founded Marseille, the oldest city in France.

The colonists came from Phocaea in what is now Turkey, their mission to establish trade links with the Gauls. They settled on the north bank of the Lacydon creek, one of the many inlets *(calanques)* that serrate the coastline. The choice was a wise one, being spread across three low hills (Butte Saint-Laurent, Butte du Panier, and Butte des Carmes) that offered protection against the Mistral, with a freshwater

Ruins of the port of Massilia in the Jardin des Vestiges

spring, and natural defence courtesy of the Frioul Archipelago. The nearby Rhône River provided the perfect means of establishing trade links with the Gauls farther inland. The settlers called the place Massalia meaning "(city) at the end of the sea" whence Marseille derives.

Massalia occupied what is today's Le Panier neighbourhood (2nd). The shoreline 2,600 years ago, however, ran farther inland, long before the Quai du Port and the Joliette Docks were created through landfill. Visible remains are few and buried deep. The Greek agora and a series of vaulted water cisterns or storerooms, for instance, have been identified beneath Place de Lenche. Nothing, however, remains of the Greek temples to Apollo, Artemis, and Athena that adorned the hilltops.

Elsewhere more has been revealed. An excavation on the Saint-Charles hill, for example, has produced evidence of the country's oldest domestic vines imported by the Greeks in 400 BC. Historians tell us that Massalia grew prosperous trading in wine and slaves. Most impressive of all are the remains of the Greek port, which in ancient times ran farther inland than it does today. They were unearthed in 1967 during the construction of the Centre Bourse shopping arcade on Rue Henri Barbusse. Today they are preserved as an archaeological park, the Jardin des Vestiges, which can be conveniently viewed from a raised walkway. A stone-edged quayside surrounding the harbour basin (now green grass) can clearly be made out, as well as three square towers and a gateway from the city wall dated to the Hellenistic period (2nd century BC). The park is part of the Marseille History Museum (Musée d'Histoire de Marseille), which sits alongside it. Here are displayed the artefacts recovered during the excavations, including a 3rd century BC trading vessel found abandoned in the silted-up harbour.

The museum also contains artefacts from the city's Roman period, which commenced in 49 BC when the city was besieged by Julius Caesar and the fleet of the Roman Republic. Massalia became Massilia but retained its Greek footprint, which it would continue to do until the time of Louis XIV (1643–1715) (see no. 9). Above-ground evidence for the Romans takes the form of a large ruined warehouse *(horreum)* at 10 Place Vivaux containing fifty large clay jars *(dolia)*, which were probably used for wine (closed at the time of writing but still visible through the windows). A large theatre has also been identified beneath Rue Saint-Laurent. The Late Romans strengthened the port with additional walls during the 5th century AD just prior to the city's capture by the Visigoths.

Other locations nearby: 2, 4, 5, 7, 8, 26

2 Songs of Revolution

Music in Marseille has often been themed around revolution. From *La Marseillaise* to hip hop, the country's second city has a powerful soundtrack all its own.

La Marseillaise was composed against the backdrop of the French Revolution (1789–1799). The profligacy of King Louis XVI (1754–1793) and his costly support of the American Revolution had brought France to the brink of bankruptcy. Add to this food shortages and fears that Louis might look to foreign intervention to shore up his flagging popularity and the stage was set for a people's revolt.

On 25th April 1792, the Mayor of Strasbourg commissioned a song "that will rally our soldiers from all over to defend their homeland that is under threat". The result was the patriotic *Chant de Guerre pour l'Armée du Rhin* (War Song for the Army of the Rhine) written by staunch royalist Claude Joseph Rouget de Lisle (1760–1836). In July, concern that such revolutionary fervour might spread prompted Austrian and Prussian forces to invade France during the War of the First Coalition. The words of the song clearly reflect French fear at the time: *Quoi! des cohortes étrangères Feraient la loi dans nos foyers! Quoi! Ces phalanges mercenaires Terrasseraient nos fiers guerriers!* (What!

Sheet music for the patriotic La Marseillaise

Foreign cohorts would make the law in our homes! What! These mercenary phalanxes would strike down our proud warriors!).

In Marseille, the song was heard for the first time on June 22nd, 1792 at the headquarters of the revolutionary Société Patriotique des Amis de la Constititution at 23–25 Rue Thubaneau (1st). There it was adopted as a marching song by the newly-formed battalion of revolutionary volunteers *(fédérés)*. Renamed *La Marseillaise*, it accompanied their march north to Paris, where in August they stormed the Tuileries Palace and apprehended the king. Thereafter the song became the first French national anthem.

In September, the Austrian and Prussian invaders were repulsed following their defeat at the Battle of Valmy. Two days later, on 21st September 1792, the French monarchy was abolished and the French First Republic declared. Since then, *La Marseillaise* has not only been appropriated as a song of revolution elsewhere, including Russia, but has also been incorporated into other pieces of music including The Beatles' *All You Need is Love*. The premises on Rue Thubaneau are now preserved as the Mémorial de la Marseillaise (currently closed for renovation).

Fast forward now to the late-20th century and equally revolutionary music is centre stage. A product largely of Marseille's immigrant communities, French hip hop is the stylised rhythmic music that accompanies spoken word rap. Marseille has thrown up many hip hop superstars, including JUL, Fonky Family, Keny Arkana, Psy 4 de la Rime, and the collective IAM, all of whom have enjoyed commercial success in the francophone world. IAM deploy their defiant, Arabic-themed rap to address social and political issues important to Muslims of the Franco-Maghrebi world, and to speak out againt racial intolerance. As early as 1991, their hit song *Les tam-tam de l'Afrique* dealt with the horrors of the Atlantic Slave Trade, the plunder of Africa, and the American plantation system.

Hip hop's first-generation rappers had ties with the Panier, Noailles, Cours Julien, and La Plaine neighbourhoods. Later it was the turn of the deprived Northern Districts *(Quartiers Nords)*, where unemployment and other social woes still fuel the music, and the Sound Musical School works to prevent delinquency through culture. And it's not only hip hop that has been engendered there. Self-taught pianist Mourad Tsimpou (2005–2024) released two remarkable albums of Classical music before his death aged just nineteen.

Other locations nearby: 1, 3, 4, 5, 6

3 Railway to the World

Secteur I (1st Arrondissement), Marseille-Saint-Charles Station (Gare de Marseille-Saint-Charles) on Square Narvik

Anyone arriving into Marseille by train, whether it be from Arles, Avignon, or farther afield, should pause at Marseille-Saint-Charles Station (Gare de Marseille-Saint-Charles). The city's main railway station, it is an impressive piece of late-19th century industrial-age architecture. Additionally, it features a colonial-era grand staircase that is a reminder of the days before air travel, when the station was the starting point for soldiers, merchants, and labourers on their way out to the colonies.

The station was born out of the need to connect Marseille to the French rail network in tandem with the modernisation of its port. No easy feat, this necessitated the excavation of the almost three-mile-long Nerthe Tunnel beneath the Étoile mountain range. Completed in 1848, with the loss of 300 lives, the tunnel carried tracks from the existing Paris–Lyon line into Marseille.

The station opened the same year. Built for the Paris to Lyon and the Mediterranean Railway Company (Compagnie des Chemins de Fer de Paris à Lyon et à la Méditerranée), it served as the southern terminus of their Paris–Marseille line and the western terminus of their Marseille–Ventimiglia line. Perched at the

Staircase to the Marseille-Saint-Charles Station

edge of a promontory, the station was initially isolated from the Old Port (Vieux Port) below. It overlooked the arterial Boulevard d'Athènes but was separated from it at the top by several buildings. Such isolation became even more of a problem when increased rail traffic saw the present station building with its huge glass roof completed in 1896.

To overcome the problem, in 1903 the buildings at the top of Boulevard d'Athènes were demolished. In their place a monumental staircase was constructed to plans by the architect Eugène Senès (1875–1960). Delayed by the Great War, it was formally inaugurated in 1927 by French President Gaston Doumergue (1863–1937).

The staircase, which connects the station with the Old Port via Boulevard d'Athènes, Boulevard Dugommier, and La Canebière, consists of 104 steps and seven landings. It is flanked by a pair of reclining female statues by Louis Botinelly (1883–1962) representing Africa and Asia (see back cover). Created as part of the 1922 Colonial Exhibition (Exposition Coloniale), they celebrated the importance of Marseille as the country's colonial gateway. Bronze sculptures of fruits, fish, harvests, and hunters by Henri Raybaud (1879–1942) represent the natural wealth of Provence. Today, the colonial-era sculptures, as well as the numerous street names in Marseille that reference former French colonies, rightly stir mixed emotions.

The station has been considerably extended since its original construction. Today, it has fourteen terminal platforms, underground parking lots, a shopping mall, and new pedestrian spaces. It handles a lot more traffic, too, as witnessed by the arrival in 2001 of the TGV, which dramatically reduced the journey time between Marseille and Northern France. As a result, annual passengers using the station increased from 7.1 million in 2000 to 16.5 million in 2017. Music fans may like to know that in 2011, American singer-songwriter Patti Smith (b. 1946) named one of the station's waiting rooms in honour of poet Arthur Rimbaud (1854–1891), who died in Marseille.

A mile or so north-east on Boulevard Isidore Dagnan (4th) stands the Marseille-Pautrier Roundhouse. Used to repair and refit steam locomotives, it retains its impressive iron truss roof by French engineer Camille Polonceau (1813–1859), with skylights to remove the smoke. A former train drivers' boarding house at 13 Rue Bénédit is now home to the Marseille Model Railway Club. Of course, their splendid layout includes a miniature version of the Marseille-Saint-Charles Station.

Other locations nearby: 2

4 Hardware, Hats and Herbs

Unfortunately, we live in an age of generic high streets and faceless out-of-town shopping malls. Idiosyncratic shops, often family-run, are increasingly a thing of the past. What a pleasure it therefore is to find a cluster of traditional, independent shops in Marseille's Noailles neighbourhood.

The first and best known is Maison Empereur at 4 Rue des Récolettes (1st). Established in 1827 in the Bourse neighbourhood, it is the oldest hardware shop in all France. The shop was named after its founder, François Empereur, a cutler by trade, hence its original focus on hardware and iron-mongery *(Ferronerie)*. In 1845, the shop moved to its present location at the bottom of the busy Rue d'Aubagne. There the business thrived and within twenty years it had expanded to include the workshop of François' son, Louis, who introduced household products *(Quincaillerie)* and culinary utensils *(Arts culinaires)*. The shop today remains in the same hands (now in the sixth generation) and its floor space has expanded to 10,000 square feet spread across several old buildings. The result is a warren of

Maison Empereur is the oldest hardware shop in France

rooms, each devoted to a different range of products whether it is cleaning products and garden tools or curtain fabrics and tin toys. Just about everything is here from wickerwork baskets and brass bells to handmade *boules* and paint brushes. The staff are knowledgeable and enthusiastic, and the experience is rounded out with a cafe-bar, museum, and archive.

Just around the corner at 5 Cours Saint-Louis is another old-fashioned shop. La Chapellerie is a traditional hat shop opened in 1924, when headgear still reflected the social status of the wearer. The shop was originally called L'Élégante and it is said that customers queued to try on the latest fashions. The marvellous *Art Nouveau* frontage remains, as does the interior woodwork and tiling. This is the place to go for your boaters, bonnets, and Borsalinos, as well as your umbrella, cane, and gloves.

One block to the south is L'Herboristerie du Père Blaize at 4 Rue Méolan et du Père Blaize, which has been purveying plant remedies and treatments since 1815. Like Maison Empereur, it remains in the hands of the same family. The shop's founder, Toussaint Blaize, exchanged his home in the Alpes de Haute-Provence for Marseille to gain better access to plants from around the world. The shop interior retains its original wood panelling, glass-fronted cabinets, and painted signboards, as well as its legion of loyal customers who appreciate the personal service and sound advice.

Other shops include: Gatimel Armurier at 28 Rue Paradis, a gun and ammunition store for hunters founded in 1830; Le Coq Gourmand at 39 Rue Fort Notre Dame, with its 18th century cellars once used to store olive oil for soap production; and Joli Rouge at 72 Rue d'Aubagne, which specialises in vintage household goods and ephemera. Finally, when you are ready for a rest, take a seat at the retro Café Prinder, founded by Italians in the 1920s at 1 Place du Marché des Capucins.

Don't forget Marseille's bookshops. Librairie Jeanne Laffitte at 25 Cours d'Estienne d'Orves (1st) is the city's oldest (1830) and most beautiful, located in part of the 17th century Galley Arsenal (Arsenal des Galères) (see no. 9). Around the corner at 10 Cours Jean Ballard is where the influential journal *Les Cahiers des Suds* was once edited. Librairie Maritime La Cardinale at nearby 26 Quai Rive Neuve (7th) offers a superb collection of seafaring titles, whilst Librairie de la Bourse at 8 Rue Paradis (1st) is good for maps and travel guides.

Other locations nearby: 1, 2, 5, 7, 8, 35

5 Story of the Stock Exchange

Secteur I (1st Arrondissement), the Palais de la Bourse at 9 La Canebière (note: the interior can only be visited during ticketed exhibitions and events)

La Canebière, the broad boulevard that runs from the Old Port (Vieux Port) out to the Réformés neighbourhood, provides central Marseille with its east–west axis. Inaugurated in 1666, when King Louis XIV (1643–1715) ordered the city's expansion, it takes its name from the Provençal *canabé* meaning 'hemp', a plant once grown locally to make ship ropes and rigging. Today it divides the city's well-to-do southern neighbourhoods from the predominantly Arab Belsunce neighbourhood to the north.

During the time of the French Third Republic (1870–1940), the Canebière became a haven for well-heeled travellers for whom luxury hotels, shops, cafés, and music halls were provided. All are gone now although there is one building from the period that still shines brightly. The flamboyant Palais de la Bourse at 9 La Canebière (1st) was completed in 1860 by the city's Chamber of Commerce and Industry. The Aix-Marseille-Provence Chamber of Commerce and Industry (CCIAMP), to give the body its full name, was the world's first chamber of commerce. Formed on 5th August 1599 by the city's elected aldermen (*échevins*), merchants, shipmasters,

Flags and columns at the Palais de la Bourse

and royal representatives, its purpose was to protect maritime trade in the Mediterranean against Barbary pirates

The Chamber was originally based in the 13th century Town Meeting House (Maison de Ville) on Quai du Port. In 1673, in line with Louis XIV's expansionist policies, this building was replaced by the City Hall (Hôtel de Ville) on the same site, rendered in flamboyant Genoese Baroque style. This building, too, was deemed inadequate – the only waterfront building to survive the Second World War, it now houses the private offices of the mayor – and was superceded by the Palais de la Bourse on La Canebière. Marseille's Chief Architect Pascal Coste (1787–1879) made sure that the new building satisfied the Chamber's desire for something that reflected Marseille's increasing commercial and colonial power. Accordingly, the building's main façade, with its imposing Corinthian columns, bears the names of eight famous explorers, whose expeditions opened the way for colonial conquests: Columbus, Cook, d'Urville, da Gama, La Pérouse, Magellan, Tasman, and Vespuce. There are also sculptures of the ancient Greek seafarers Euthymenes and Pytheas, both of whom lived in Marseille, and the roof is crowned with a sculpture depicting the city's arms.

Inside the entrance a marble staircase leads to administrative offices, as well as a huge central trading floor designed to hold 2,500 traders. This is surrounded by eighteen arcaded brokers' offices, where visitors could mingle at will. Each arcade is inscribed with the name of one of Marseille's colonial-era trading partners, including Egypt, Indochina, Portugal, and Tunisia. Relief panels on the ceiling depict the foundation of Marseille, the conquest of Algeria, the start of the Crusades, and various scientific expeditions. Emperor Napoleon III (1808–1873), who did much to modernise the French economy, laid the building's foundation stone.

The Palais de la Bourse today functions as a labour history archive, with almost 2.5 miles of shelving, as well as an exhibition space, which can be visited during ticketed events. The surrounding terrace is home to a restaurant, a pair of rusting ships' anchors, and a Marseille-made COMEX divers' decompression chamber.

Directly opposite the Old Stock Exchange is a signpost marking the spot where on 9th October 1934, King Alexander I of Yugoslavia (1888–1934) was assassinated by a Macedonian nationalist. The king had been in Marseille on a state visit to cement relations with France in the face of Italian aggression. French Foreign Minister Louis Barthou (1862–1934) was also fatally wounded.

Other locations nearby: 1, 2, 4, 7, 8, 26

6 Tragedy on Rue d'Aubagne

Secteur I (1st arrondissement), the 2018 building collapse at 63 and 65 Rue d'Aubagne

Monday 5th November 2018 started like any other day on Marseille's Rue d'Aubagne. It was 9am and people were either getting ready for the day or else still sleeping. Then tragedy struck. Two dilapidated buildings at numbers 63 and 65 suddenly collapsed, causing the death of eight occupants. The story of that day, and of the days that followed, revealed much about a city at the cusp of ruin and revival.

At the time of the collapse, the building at number 63, which belonged to a mixed economy company called Marseille Habitat, was unoccupied. By contrast, number 65 was an inhabited condominium, which is where the deaths occurred. After attending to the victims, the emergency services immediately demolished the unoccupied building at number 67, which had been dangerously weakened.

Caught by surprise, the Municipality was unprepared for such an event. In the months following the disaster they took stock of the city's older housing and identified no less than 578 dangerous buildings, a third of which stood near the collapsed properties on Rue

A gaping hole where houses once stood on Rue d'Aubagne

d'Aubagne. Some 4,500 people were evacuated from these buildings and relocated to hotels. Three years later, 1,500 of them were still living in temporary accommodation.

The tragedy on Rue d'Aubagne revealed in the worst possible way the failings within the Municipality's urban planning and housing departments. The housing associations *Un Centre-ville pour Tous* and *Collectif du 5 Novembre* blamed the tragedy on the Municipality's policy of encouraging gentrification in the city centre, whilst failing to invest in properties occupied by the less wealthy. The Municipality under incumbent mayor Jean-Claude Gaudin (1939–2024) responded by blaming heavy rain, unscrupulous private landlords, and administrative inertia. Against this backdrop, six elected officials of the Republican Party were accused of either renting or selling unsanitary and unsafe housing in Marseille.

In June 2020, a judicial investigation into the collapse revealed that it had been caused by the failure of a prop supporting the ground floor of the inhabited building at number 65. Experts on the matter pointed their fingers at major failings in building maintenance on the part of the Municipality, as well as various private bodies, which had been informed of the building's failing fabric since 2014. Indictments of guilty parties followed in November 2020. They included that of Marseille Habitat (the owner of the empty building at number 63), Julien Ruas (the deputy in charge of Jean-Claude Gaudin's risk management and prevention service), Richard Carta (an expert who visited the occupied property at number 65 just a few days prior to the tragedy), and of the limited liability company Liautard (the trustee in charge of the property at number 65 in which the victims had lived). None of the property owners were indicted at the time.

At the same time, a group founded by the public prosecutor's office to investigate substandard housing presented its findings, which resulted in prison terms for several Marseille slum traders and identified thousands of city properties deemed liable to collapse. At the time of writing, the trial of those suspected of being responsible for the Rue d'Aubagne collapses is ongoing.

Since the tragedy on Rue d'Aubagne, the site where the buildings stood has been cleared and left empty. Locals call it the Hollow Tooth. Plans are afoot to create something special here, financed by the City of Marseille and consisting of a multi-use public building, a memorial space, and a Mediterranean patio. Until then, several makeshift memorials tell the tragic tale.

Other locations nearby: 4, 5, 7, 35

7 An Art Deco Opera House

Secteur I (1st Arrondissement), the Opéra Municipal at 2 Rue Molière

The twentieth century was hard on the entertainment venues of Marseille. The gradual decline of the city's commercial fortunes was reflected in the loss of its 19th century theatres and music halls, notably along the arterial Canebière (1st). The Gymnase, Palais de Cristal, and Variétés (now a cinema) were all victims, as were the *Grand Cafés* that supported them. Also lost was the Alhambra-inspired Théâtre de l'Alcazar at 58 Cours Belsunce, and with it a colourful local audience that included dockers, white-collar workers, and seamen in transit. Opened in 1857, it was converted into a cinema in the 1930s, and subsequently demolished leaving only the canopied doorway, which since 2004 has provided access to a municipal library.

Fortunately, Marseille's Municipal Opera (Opéra Municipal) at 2 Rue Molière (1st) has fared better. The city's first opera house was inaugurated in 1685 being only the second provincial French opera house after Bordeaux. This was replaced in 1787 by the neo-

An Art Deco detail at the Opéra Municipal

Classical Grand-Théâtre, which stood where the current opera now stands on land freed up by the demolition of the Galley Arsenal (Arsenal des Galères) (see no. 9). During the 19th century, it was the setting for performances of *Lucia di Lammermoor* and *Il Barbiere di Siviglia* given by the Italian soprano, Adelina Patti (1843–1919), whom composer Giuseppe Verdi (1813–1901) described as being a "stupendous artist".

In November 1919, following the installation of electricity, the opera house was gutted by fire. Only the outer walls, box office, and front colonnade were left standing. Of these, only the box office and colonnade were retained when the opera house was rebuilt by local architect Gaston Castel (1886–1971). Reopened in 1924, the box office is located in the centre of the entrance hall from which two staircases rise to the elegant main foyer. Seating for 1,823 is spread across a classic fan-shaped auditorium, with two balconies and a gallery terminated by loggias. An impressive frieze called *La Naissance de la Beauté* depicting Aphrodite flanked by comic and tragic masks frames the stage. It is the work of French sculptor Antoine Bourdelle (1861–1929), who a decade earlier had provided decoration for the Théâtre des Champs-Élysées in Paris, which heralded the debut of the *Art Deco* style. In his book *Opera Houses of the World* (1996), musicologist Thierry Beauvert describes the Marseille Opera as "an Art Deco temple".

Far from being the preserve of the local élite, opera in Marseille was from the start a favourite entertainment of the masses. The proximity to Italy and presence of a significant Italian community meant that certain operatic works were heard in Marseille before Paris, including Bellini's *Norma* and Verdi's *Le Trouvère*. Such fervour sustained the populace during the Second World War, with touring companies hosted throughout the German Occupation (1942–1944). It also helps explain why opera survived in Marseille but the music halls did not, and why several well-known modern singers have chosen Marseille to make their French debuts, including Plácido Domingo (b. 1941), Renata Scotto (1934–2023), and Alfredo Kraus (1927–1999). Not that they will always have had an easy ride since Marseille is known for its knowledgeable and at times critical audience.

Close by the Opera, at 46 Rue Francis Davso, is the venerable Cafés Debout. Opened in 1932, it originally sold not only coffee but also oil and soap, both staples of the Marseillais economy. Excellent coffee is roasted on the premises today, with a variety of fine teas also available.

Other locations nearby: 1, 2, 4, 5, 6, 8, 9

8 Catch of the Day

Secteur I (1st arrondissement), the Old Port Fish Market (Marché aux Poissons du Vieux Port) at 1 Quai de la Fraternité (formerly Quai des Belges) (note: as with all street markets it is best to arrive early for the best selection)

Marseille is a working city, with a host of street markets popular with locals. That is not to say that visitors are not welcome, however, indeed it would be a shame not to experience these snapshots of native colour.

One of the best is the Old Port Fish Market (Marché aux Poissons du Vieux Port) held several mornings a week at 1 Quai de la Fraternité (formerly Quai des Belges) (1st). A Marseille institution, this is where local fishermen sell their catch from the rocky coves *(calanques)* around Marseille (see no. 42). Until 1976 they would have been found alongside commercial trawlermen at the Criée, the fish auction hall on Quai de Rive Neuve, which has since been converted into a theatre. Wholesale auctions are now held at Port de Saumaty near L'Estaque in the north.

It helps to have knowledge of the names of the fish on sale, and their Provençal equivalents. Easy to identify is the ray-finned Red Scorpionfish (Provençal *Chapon/Rascasse)*, which together with European Conger Eel *(Congre)*, and Sea Robin *(Grondin)*, provides the basic ingredient for Marseille's famous *Bouillabaisse* (see no. 15). Other species include Red Gurnard *(Rouget Grondin)*, Monkfish *(Lotte/Baudroie)*, John Dory *(Saint-Pierre)*, Gilthead Bream *(Dorade)*, Whiting *(Mer-*

A fine display at the Old Port Fish Market

lan), Red Mullet *(Galinette)*, and Weever *(Vive)*. There are also plenty of shellfish, including crabs, lobsters, and sea urchins. It might be disturbing for some visitors to see fishtails still flapping as they are deposited into customers' shopping bags!

A good day to attend the Fish Market is on a Saturday morning, when it is accompanied by a colourful flower market. This is laid out beneath British architect Norman Foster's mirror pavilion, known locally as *L'Ombrière*, which consists of a 130 feet long polished steel mirror set on slender tubular stilts. The inverted reflection of both flowers and punters makes for one of the city's most photographed locations.

A different but no less representative market takes place on Rue d'Aubagne (6th), one of several busy streets that run down into the city from the surrounding hills. The shops here once specialised in furniture and jewellery for the original bourgeois population. Today, like many streets in the Noailles neighbourhood, they have been replaced by shops and restaurants selling African and Asian produce. The frenetic daily Marché Noailles on Place du Marché des Capucins, which opened in 1956, is where immigrants from the Maghreb buy their exotic fruits, halal meat, flatbread, and Tunisian pastries. The spice dealer Le Paradies d'Épices at 34 and the Mama Africa Ivorian restaurant at 57 are typical, as are the Tam-Ky Asian supermarket at 5 Rue Halle Delacroix and the Pâtisserie Orientale Maison Journo at 28 Rue de Pavillon. Restaurant Fémina at 1 Rue du Musée has been serving the best barley couscous since 1921.

Other good produce and flower markets are held weekly on Cours Julien/Place Jean Jaurès and Avenue du Prado (both 6th), whilst antique and vintage collectors will enjoy the huge covered market at 130 Chemin de la Madrague-Ville (15th). A unique market hall is the Halle Puget on Rue Halle Puget (1st). Built in 1672 for butchers and fishmongers in the style of a Greek temple, it later served as a chapel. It is used today by local market gardeners to sell their homegrown produce.

"C'est la sardine qui a bouché le port de Marseille" (The sardine that choked the port of Marseille) is an old expression denoting the supposed tendency of the Marseillais to exaggerate. It dates from the 18th century, when a British ship named *Sartine* sank in the mouth of the harbour.

Other locations nearby: 1, 4, 5, 7, 9, 26

9 The Lost Galley Shipyard

Secteur I (1st Arrondissement), a tour of what remains of the Galley Arsenal (Arsenal des Galères) around Place Thiars

One of the liveliest parts of Marseille's Old Port (Vieux Port) is the gridiron of streets around Place Thiars (1st). Bounded by the Quai de Rive Neuve, Rue Breteuil, Rue Sainte, and Rue Fort Notre-Dame, the area buzzes with restaurants, cafés, bars, and shops. It is difficult to imagine that here once stood the galley shipyard of King Louis XIV (1638–1715).

Marseille was founded as a trading post in 600BC by Greek colonists. They chose the Lacydon creek, one of the many rocky inlets *(calanques)* that serrate the coastline. The walled settlement rose on the creek's northern shore in the area known today as Le Panier. Its dock facilities at the far eastern end of the creek have been revealed by archaeologists and are now part of the Marseille History Museum (Musée d'Histoire de Marseille) (see no. 1).

It was the Romans who were first to build a galley shipyard, which formed a separate military enclave on the creek's southern shore. The ten galleys based there, which were loyal to Pompey (106–48 BC),

An engraving of 1738 showing the Galley Arsenal of Louis XIV in the foreground

failed to prevent Julius Caesar (100–44 BC) from taking Massalia in 49 BC. The galleys used by both sides relied on oars for propulsion, their slender hulls, shallow draft, and low freeboard developed specifically for use in Mediterranean warfare.

Throughout Antiquity and the Middle Ages the city retained its footprint on the northern shore. The galley shipyard, however, was rebuilt and relocated as necessary. Thus during the 13th century the Counts of Provence, and later King Charles IV (1294–1328), used a shipyard at the eastern end of the creek. This continued into the 15th century with Charles VIII (1470–1498), who built galleys for the Italian Wars. During the same century, timbers reclaimed from a retired galley were used to build the church in which Henri II (1519–1559) married Catherine de' Medici (1519–1589), on a site occupied today by the 16th century Church of Saint-Ferréol les Augustins at 9 Rue Reine Elisabeth. Galley production peaked under Henri, with a record of 42 galleys built.

By the time of Louis XIV (1638–1715), Marseille was no longer home to a war fleet. Louis, however, still demanded a fleet that outshone those of Spain and Italy. Accordingly, in 1665 he ordered the city walls be extended to accommodate a new galley shipyard (the line of this extension is marked in the pavement of Place Charles de Gaulle) (see no. 13). His First Minister of State, Jean-Baptiste Colbert (1619–1683), oversaw construction of what became known as the Galley Arsenal (Arsenal des Galères). Completed in 1690, its huge L-shaped footprint filled the south-eastern corner of the port between the present Palais de la Bourse and Rue du Fort Notre-Dame. It included six galley docks, a hospital, lumber yard, rope workshop, rigging stores, and an armoury containing 10,000 muskets. In all, some 20,000 men resided at the Arsenal, around a fifth of the population at the time.

The forty galleys stationed in Marseille were each manned by 260 slaves, most of whom were common law convicts. Known as *galériens*, they were branded with the letters *GAL* and shackled to their vessels for campaigns of two to three months at a time. Barefoot, and with minimal rations, half of them died during their period of servitude.

By the end of Louis' reign the use of galleys in naval warfare had given way to sailing ships. Consequently in 1748, Louis XV (1710–1774) ceased all galley construction. The Arsenal, which had been in operation barely a century, was sold to the City and by 1787 it had been demolished. This allowed several roads to be extended down to the quayside, notably La Canebière. The galley docks were infilled and replaced by eight new Italianate building blocks centred on Place

Thiars, and the whole surrounded by a customs canal. The Old Port's shallow depth, however, was a barrier to modern merchant shipping and so between 1844 and 1853, the deeper basins of the Joliette Docks were opened to the north-west.

In 1927, the canal was infilled and in its place the roads so popular with today's revellers were laid. And these are not the only reminders of the former Arsenal: the imposing building at 23 Cours Honoré d'Estienne d'Orves known as *La Capitainerie* was the harbour-master's office; the building next door at 25 was the Arsenal headquarters; the three blocks at Rue Sainte 34–68 occupy the footprint of the convicts' rope-making workshop; and the three staircases on Rue Fortia, Rue de la Paix Marcel Paul, and Place aux Huiles were built to allow access down to the Arsenal, which was built at sea level.

A sculpture recalling the Galley Arsenal

The Old Port, once key to Marseille's prosperity, today serves as a marina and a terminus for local ferries. The Joliette Docks, worked until 1988, now lie at the heart of a new cultural and business quarter called the Euroméditerranée Zone (see no. 21). They in turn have largely given way to the massive Grand Port Maritime de Marseille, which runs northwards all the way to L'Estaque, with satellite extensions around Fos-sur-Mer and the **Étang** de Berre. To discover more about their history visit the Musée de la Réparation Navale at 7 Boulevard des Bassins de Radoub.

Other locations nearby: 5, 7, 8, 10

10 The Santons of Provence

Secteur I (7th Arrondissement), the Ateliers Marcel Carbonel – Santons & Art de Vivre Provençal at 47 Rue Neuve Sainte Catherine (note: workshop is only open mid-Jan–mid-Jul & Sep Wed 9am–1pm, 2–5pm; shop Mon–Fri 9am–1pm, 2–6pm & Sat 10am–1pm, 2–6pm)

An important part of any Provençal Christmas is the creation of a Nativity crib. Unlike elsewhere, a Provençal crib is special in that not only is the Holy Family depicted but also a host of secular characters, too. These hand-crafted figures are known as *santons*, from the Provençal *santoun* meaning 'little saint', and those who make them are *santonniers*.

The *santon* story goes back to the 13th century, and the staging of a life-sized Nativity by Saint Francis of Assisi. Later, during the 17th century, a Capuchin monk in Marseille created miniature figurines for people to create their own Nativity scenes at home. These grew in popularity during the French Revolution, when churches were closed and Nativity scenes forbidden. Finally, in the mid-19th century, secular figures derived from the *Pastorale Maurel*, a Provençal-language Nativity play by Marseille-born writer Antoine Maurel (1815–1897), were added.

Originally families made their *santons* from whatever materials they had to hand, including wax, plaster, *papier-mâché*, and even breadcrumbs. The professional *santonnier*, however, uses clay. To appreciate the *santonnier's* craft one should take a tour of the Ateliers Marcel Carbonel at 47 Rue Neuve Sainte Catherine (7th Arrondissement). Marseille's premier *santon* workshop, it was founded in 1935 and has been recognised since 2007 as an Entreprise du Patrimoine Vivant (Living Heritage Company).

Each *santon* character, whether it is an old woman sitting on a stone wall or Jesus himself, begins life as a detailed clay model. A two-part plaster mold is then created from the model. Clay can then be pressed into the mold time and again to generate exact copies of the original. Next the *santon* is deburred and left to dry. It is then individually stamped by the *santonnier* and fired for a day in an oven above 980°C. The *santon* is now ready for painting using opaque watercolours (*gouache*), with acrylics for some details. Ateliers Marcel Carbonel is the last company to employ a full-time employee to create its own colours, namely 300 different shades hand-mixed from fifteen basic pigments.

After the tour, visitors can peruse a selection of finished *santons* in the company shop and purchase those they like. Many traditional Provençal characters are represented, including the miller, shepherd, priest, garlic merchant, faggot seller, washerwoman, and fisherman, as well as specific characters such as the *ravi* (the village fool who raises his arms in delight), the *Arlesienne* in her beautiful dress, and a young girl with a bouquet of lavender. In total the company manufactures more than 1,300 different figures in six different sizes!

A separate page on the company's website (www.marcelcarbonel.com) gives

All santons at Marcel Carbonel are painted carefully by hand

full details on how to create your own Provençal Nativity scene once you get your *santons* home. Regarding the creation of a suitable backdrop, it should be noted that the Holy Family is ideally placed to one side so as to create room for the procession of villagers as they pass through a 19th century Provençal village to converge on the lowly barn. According to tradition, the Nativity scene is displayed until Candlemas Day on February 2nd.

Santons are also out in force during the annual Santon Fair, which starts on the last Sunday in November on either Place Général De Gaulle or Quai du Port (1st). The fair is preceded by a Santonniers' Mass at the neo-Gothic Les Réformés Church at 8 Cours Franklin Roosevelt (1st Arrondissement). The name of the church recalls a Chapel of Reformed Augustinians that once stood on the same site.

Other locations nearby: 9, 11, 12, 13

11 A Game of Tanned Feet

Some fifteen and a half miles east of Marseille is the coastal town of La Ciotat. In 1895, it was the setting for one of the first projected motion pictures, the Lumière brothers' 50-second *L'Arrivée d'un Train en Gare de La Ciotat*. It is also where in 1907 the quintessentially Provençal game of *pétanque* was invented.

The origins of *pétanque* go back to the Romans, when an early version of the ball-tossing game known today as *boules* was imported into Roman Gaul. It involved players competing to throw a stone ball *(boule)* as near as possible to a target embedded in the ground. By the Middle Ages, stone balls had been replaced by wooden ones, and by the 19th century the game had become popular throughout France.

In the South of France, the game was known as *Jeu de Boules Provençal*, in which players rolled their *boule*, or else ran three steps before throwing their *boule*, as recorded in the novels of Marcel Pagnol (1895–1974) (see no. 46). Unfortunately for La Ciotat resident Jules Lenoir, however, this more energetic version was off limits because of his arthritis. Instead, he conjured up a version of *boules* in which the player's feet remained firmly in one spot. This explains the origin of the name *pétanque*, which derives from *Jeu de Boules Pieds Tanqués* (literally 'Boules with Feet Anchored'), and why it is known as the game of tanned feet! The first ever *pétanque* tournament was staged in La Ciotat in 1910.

Typically, a *pétanque* court is a level, rectangular area of flattened open ground. One of many in Marseille is the Boulodrome Jardin du Carénage near 47 Quai de Rive Neuve (7th Arrondissement). With stone steps for spectators shaded by rows of mulberry trees and oleander bushes, the court has as its backdrop the fortified Abbey of Saint Victor (Abbaye Saint-Victor) (see no. 12). On a warm summer's day, this is a good place to appreciate the mechanics of *pétanque*. Played by two, four, or six people in two teams, the starting team make a circle on the ground from where all players must throw their *boules* (today made of steel). The first player throws a smaller wooden jack ball called a *cochonnet* ('piglet') and then the first *boule*. An opposing player then makes a throw, and

A game of pétanque at the Boulodrome Jardin du Carénage

play continues with the team farthest from the jack continuing to throw until they land nearer the jack than their opponents, or until they run out of *boules*. Play continues with a player from the winning team making a new circle where the jack finished, and then throwing the jack for a new game. Play ends and points are scored when both teams have no more *boules*, or when the jack is knocked out of play. The winning team receives a point for each *boule* it has closer to the jack than the best-placed *boule* of the opposition. If the jack is knocked out of play, no points are awarded unless one team has *boules* left to play, in which case the team receives a point for each *boule* left. The first team to reach 13 points wins. Despite such apparent complexities, *pétanque* is played enthusiastically by around seventeen million people.

Visitors seduced by the game should visit the Maison de la Boule, a dedicated museum at 4 Place Des 13 Cantons (2nd Arrondissement), and perhaps even the Boule Bleue Factory at 57 Montée de Saint-Menet (11th Arrondissement), where *boules* have been manufactured since 1904. For Marseille's only underground *pétanque* court visit the restaurant Le République at 1 Place Sadi-Carnot (2nd).

Other locations nearby: 9, 10, 12, 13

12 The Abbey of Saint Victor

Secteur I (7th Arrondissement), the Abbey of Saint Victor (Abbaye Saint-Victor) on Place Saint-Victor

During the Middle Ages there was a place at the bottom of La Canebière where ships' hulls were turned, cleaned, and re-caulked. In French this process is known as *carénage*. In 1840, with the increase in commercial shipping into the Old Port (Vieux Port), a new Bassin de Carénage was created at the far end of the Quai Rive Neuve. It is still there today albeit now used as a marina for pleasure boats (see front cover). The new basin was cut from the living rock, the same rock that had been quarried in ancient Greek times for building materials and sarcophagi. Evidence for this has been found beneath the Abbey of Saint Victor (Abbaye Saint-Victor), which overlooks the basin.

The crypt beneath the Abbey of Saint Victor

The Abbey of Saint Victor was established in 415 AD by the Christian monk and theologian John Cassian (360–435). After spending many years studying monasticism in the Middle East, in Marseille he created a cenobitic monastic complex for both men and women, one of the first in the West. He named it in honour of Victor, a Roman army officer in Marseille, who was executed in 290 AD for refusing to denounce the worship of idols.

Thereafter, the abbey had a tumultuous history. During the 5th century, the monks were accused of heresy for following Cassian and the Desert Fathers in their belief that man could by his own powers convert to Christianity. Later, in 838, the monastery was destroyed by a Saracen fleet. The then-abbess, Saint Eusebia, was martyred along with thirty-nine nuns.

In 977, monastic life was restored under the Rule of Saint Benedict. The community was led by a series of inspirational abbots, including a Catalan monk named Isarn (d. 1048), who rebuilt the abbey, and Guillaume Grimoard (1310–1370), who in 1361 became Pope Urban V. He added the high crenellated walls, so important considering the monastery was located outside the city. Thereafter, however, the abbey went into decline, especially during the 16th century, when commendatory abbots drew revenues without controlling internal discipline. The failure of the monks to provide aid during the Great Plague of 1720 prompted Marseille's aldermen (échevins) to have the abbey secularised. By the time of the French Revolution, the abbey was closed, stripped of its treasures, and being used as a barn, prison, and barracks.

All that remains of the abbey today is the rebuilt abbey church although its interior is stark. Instead, the real highlight is the large and atmospheric crypt, which occupies not only the ancient quarry but also the site of the original monastery church. It contains numerous tombs, including Abbot Isarn's grave slab cut from the base of an ancient sarcophagus, his head and feet peeping out from beneath a long inscription.

On the feast of Candlemas *(Chandeleur)* (2nd February), Marseille's archbishop makes a candlelit pilgrimage to the crypt, where he blesses a miracle-working statue known as Our Lady of the Confession of the Martyrs, or the Black Virgin for short. He then proceeds along Rue Sainte to Four des Navettes, Marseille's oldest bakery (1781). There he blesses boat-shaped orange blossom biscuits inspired by the vessel that some believe brought the Biblical Mary Magdalene to Marseille, along with Christianity.

In 2016, another ancient Greek quarry *(Carrière antique)* was discovered between nearby Rue des Lices and Boulevard de la Corderie. Lying alongside an extension of the city wall commissioned in 1666 by Louis XIV ((1638–1715)), it contains half-quarried sarcophagi, abandoned after faults in the stone were discovered. The site has been reburied for protection.

Other locations nearby: 10, 11, 13, 14, 15

13 A Tale of Two Forts

Secteur I (7th Arrondissement), Fort Saint Nicholas (Fort Saint-Nicolas) at 2 Boulevard Charles Livon

Two forts stand sentinel at the entrance to Marseille's Old Port (Vieux Port). To the north is Fort Saint John (Fort Saint-Jean) (2nd), with its two towers, whilst across the water to the south is the star-shaped Fort Saint Nicholas (Fort Saint-Nicolas) (7th). Both dating from the late-17th century, they were commissioned by King Louis XIV (1638–1715) not only to defend the port but also to keep a watchful eye on the city following a series of council-led revolts. Although a part of the Kingdom of France since 1486, Marseille retained an autonomous status. The construction of the forts represented the city's defeat as a separate entity.

Fort Saint Nicholas was completed in 1664 to a plan by military engineer Louis Nicolas de Clerville (1610–1677). Located on high ground behind the Abbey of Saint Victor (Abbaye Saint-Victor), it occupies the former site of a 12th century chapel dedicated to Saint Nicholas. Known as the Citadelle de Marseille, the fort included a line of cannon pointed directly at the city. No wonder the Marseillais tried to destroy the fort during the French Revolution! Later,

An aerial view of Fort Saint Nicholas known as the Citadelle

in 1860, by which time the fort was redundant and serving as a prison, it was cut in half by the new Boulevard Charles Livon, leaving part of the structure marooned on the shoreline. In 2024, after being closed to the public for 360 years, the upper part of Fort Saint Nicholas (known as Fort d'Entrecasteaux) opened to visitors. The great angular bastions can now be viewed up close, and the ramparts can be climbed to where a new landscape garden and some wonderful views await.

Fort Saint John is built on lower ground occupied during the late-12th century by the Commandery of the Military Order of the Knights Hospitaller of Saint John. From here they dispatched troops to the Holy Land. The Knights' chapel, which survives, was incorporated into the fort's fabric, as were two towers: the square Tour du Roi René built in the 15th century by the Count of Provence to guard the port, and the circular Tour du Fanal built in 1644 as a watchtower and fire beacon (see back cover). The fort in its present iteration was completed in 1660 again to a plan by Clerville.

In April 1790, Fort Saint John was seized by a revolutionary mob. During the subsequent period of revolutionary rule, it too served as a prison, its most famous inmate being Louis Philippe II (1747–1793), Duke of Orléans, who spent several months here before being sent to Paris, where despite his support for the Revolution he was executed.

During the 19th and 20th centuries, Fort Saint John served as a French Army barracks and a stopover for Foreign Legion recruits on their way to Algeria. Occupied during the Second World War by the Germans, it was badly damaged by the explosion of an ammunition depot. Later restored, in 2013 it became a part of the new Museum of European and Mediterranean Civilisations (Musée des Civilisations de l'Europe et de la Méditerranée) (MuCEM) to which it is linked by an aerial walkway (see no. 21). A second footbridge connects the fort with the forecourt of the Church of Saint-Laurent on the edge of Le Panier (see no. 25).

The Tour du Roi René originally contained the Old Port's health office, which worked to prevent the arrival of ship-borne epidemics. In 1717, it relocated to the neo-Classical Consigne Sanitaire pavilions on the nearby Quai du Port. They are currently being renovated for use as a centre for the promotion of the Mediterannean as a sustainable urban resource.

Other locations nearby: 11, 12, 13, 14, 16

14 The Palais du Pharo

Secteur I (7th Arrondissement), the Palais du Pharo and park at 58 Boulevard Charles Livon

For a superb view of the Old Port (Vieux Port), not to mention the fireworks on Bastille Day (14th July), one should head up to the Pharo headland. Located above Fort Saint Nicholas, it is dominated today by the Palais du Pharo. The name, however, betrays an earlier structure, a 14th century lighthouse (ancient Greek *pharos*), which guided shipping into the port below.

The palace dates from the mid-19th century, a time when Marseille was flourishing due to the growth of its maritime trade and colonies. Instrumental in this was Louis-Napoléon Bonaparte (1808–1873), who ruled France as the last French Emperor, Napoleon III. He helmed a major upgrade of the city's infrastructure, which included the new Joliette Docks (see no. 9). In return, the City of Marseille gifted him the Pharo headland on which to build a summer residence.

The Palais du Pharo is based on the Villa Eugénie, another imperial residence built around the same time in Biarritz. It is oriented so as to best resist the strong northwesterly Mistral. Construction began in 1858 but was delayed due to a shortage of stone (the city's Cathedral was built at the same time) and a change of architect (the project was started by Hector-Martin Lefuel (1810–1880), known for his work on the Louvre). By 1870, when it was completed under Henri-Jacques Espérandieu (1829–1874), the fall of the Second French Empire was only a year away, and Napoleon never moved in.

The incoming Third French Republic saw Bonapartist symbols removed from the palace. It also brought with it a lawsuit by the now-widowed former Empress Eugénie for the return of the palace. In 1884, she won her case and donated the building to the City of Marseille on condition it be used for the public good. As a result, in 1893, at the instigation of renowned pharmacist Édouard Marie Heckel (1843–1916), it became home to the city's medical school, which relocated here from the Pavillon Daviel in Le Panier (see no. 27).

Later, in 1903, the old palace served as a cholera and tuberculosis hospital, as well as a medical school for colonial troops, which evolved into a military institute of tropical medicine. Then, in 1930, the medical school became a university faculty, where by the time

The Palais du Pharo sits on a headland jutting into the sea

of its closure in 2013 some eight thousand doctors and pharmacists were trained. Several are remembered in nearby street names, including the inventor of the rabies vaccine Louis Pasteur (1822–1895), hospital administrator Charles Livon (1850–1917), sleeping sickness expert Eugène Jamot (1879–1937), and epidemiologist Paul-Louis Simond (1858–1947).

The Palais du Pharo is now a conference centre. Although not freely accessible to the public, the surrounding park is open daily. Named for the microbiologist Émile Duclaux (1840–1904), who succeeded Louis Pasteur at his namesake institute in Marseille, it contains the *Monument to Heroes and Victims of the Sea* (1923), which depicts three sailors in a lifeboat snagged on a reef. There is also a series of eighty-four rusty steel arches known collectively as *Désordre* (Disorder) by the conceptualist sculptor Bernard Venet (b. 1941).

In the cove beneath the Palace is the Borg Shipyard (Chantier Naval Borg). Established in 1956 by the son of an Italian shipwright, it specialises in the construction and re-fitting of Marseille *barquettes*, small wooden boats designed to navigate the Bay of Marseille. Used for centuries under sail by fishermen, since the 1920s they have increasingly been motorised for use as pleasure craft.

Other locations nearby: 13, 15, 16, 17

15 Boiled and then Simmered

Secteur I (7th Arrondissement), Chez Michel at 6 Rue des Catalans (note: dining hours are limited so booking is strongly recommended)

If there is one traditional dish that defines Marseille it is *Bouillabaisse*. Pronounced *boo-ya-bess*, the exact origins of this rich fish soup are unclear. Historians tell us that the ancient Greek colonists who founded Marseille in 600 BC ate a plain fish broth known as *kakavia*. *Bouillabaisse*, however, is a relatively complex affair, so it is undoubtedly a more recent invention. It is said that it came about when local fishermen, sorting their catch for market, set aside pieces of bony fish to cook later at home. Over the years, what started as a basic family stew morphed into today's *Bouillabaisse*.

What sets *Bouillabaisse* apart from other Mediterannean fish soups is the choice of bony Mediterranean coastal fish, the method of cooking, the use of Provençal herbs, and the way finished soup is served separately from the fish. Recipes for *Bouillabaisse* have long been a topic for discussion, with chefs disputing which is the most authentic. In 1980, a group of Marseille restaurateurs drew up a *Bouillabaisse* Charter, which codified the correct ingredients and method of preparation. Accordingly, an authentic Marseille *Bouillabaisse* should include at least four different fresh fish from the rocky coves *(calanques)* around Marseille: Red Scorpionfish; European Conger Eel; Sea Robin; and shellfish such as crabs, lobsters, or sea urchins (see no. 8). However, since it

The author enjoying Bouillabaisse at Chez Michel

depends on what fish is available on the day, a chef might substitute Red Gurnard, Monkfish, John Dory, Gilthead Bream, Whiting, Red Mullet, and Weever. Either way, the chef should ideally use a combination of lean, firm-fleshed, and gelatinous fish.

First the fish are cleaned with seawater, scaled, and sliced. Next olive oil is poured into a large casserole, with sliced onions, crushed garlic, and peeled tomatoes. This mixture is browned on a low heat for about five minutes after which the fish is added, firm pieces first. The fish are then covered with water, as well as fennel, saffron, thyme, bay, cayenne pepper, and seasoning, and brought to the boil. It is then simmered before the next more delicate pieces of fish are added. It is this process of boiling and simmering to ensure that all the fish is equally well cooked that explains the word *Bouillabaisse*, which is a compound of two Provençal verbs: *bolhir* (to boil) and *abaissar* (to reduce).

The soup is now left to cook for about twenty minutes, during which a pan of peeled potatoes is boiled. A spicy mayonnaise called *rouille* is also prepared from egg yolk, olive oil, crushed garlic, cayenne pepper, and saffron, and spread onto thick slices of rustic bread. Finally, the fish is removed from the soup, which is served piping hot, with the bread floating on top. The fish and potatoes are served as a separate course.

Restaurants serving good *Bouillabaisse* include Le Miramar at 12 Quai du Port (2nd), Le Rhul at 269 Corniche Kennedy (7th), and Chez Fonfon at 140 Rue du Vallon des Auffes (7th). This author enjoyed an excellent *Bouillabaisse* courtesy of Chez Michel at 6 Rue des Catalans (7th), where the Visciano family has been serving the dish since 1946.

For a modern take on Marseille's seafood tradition visit La Boîte à Sardine at 2 Boulevard de la Libération (1st), where octopus sausages *(caillettes)* and cheese-stuffed sardines are served amidst all manner of nauticalia.

Not to be confused with *Bouillabaisse* is *Bourride*. This is made from fish filets cooked in a soup, which is then enriched with egg yolks and *aioli* (garlic and olive oil) whisked in at the last moment.

Other locations nearby: 13, 14, 16, 17

16 Along the Kennedy Corniche

Secteur I (7th Arrondissement), a walk along the Corniche du Président-John-Fitzgerald-Kennedy beginning at Plage des Catalans

The sandy Catalans Beach (Plage des Catalans), just beyond the Palais du Pharo, marks the start of the Corniche du Président-John-Fitzgerald-Kennedy. Named in 1963 following the US President's assassination, and known locally as *La Corniche*, it runs south along the Mediterranean coast as far as Plage du Prado. Along the way it takes in many interesting locations, and some glorious views out to the Frioul Archipelago (Îles du Frioul) (see no. 20).

Beginning in 1863 as a narrow coastal path, the Corniche only became a real road in 1954. During the intervening years, a tram line came this way, although this was later removed to make way for motor vehicles. Since 2021, the Corniche has been closed to road traffic on one Sunday each month.

Our first port of call is the eyecatching Hôtel Le Péron. Completed in 1931, it features a wealth of *Art Deco* detailing. The hotel restaurant across the road clings precariously to the rocky shoreline. On the next headland stands the impressive Monument to the Fallen of the Army of the Orient and Distant Lands (Monument aux Morts de l'Armée d'Orient et des Terres Lointaines). Erected in 1927, it was originally intended to honour the French Expeditionary Force, which fought in Bulgaria, Hungary, Russia, and Turkey. A later dedication honours the soldiers of all faiths who died for France in North Africa and Indochina. In the form of a huge gateway, it contains a bronze *Victory* figure flanked by goddesses of war and sea.

Adjacent is a three-arched viaduct, which crosses the Vallons des Auffes, *l'auffe* being the perennial Esparto Grass *(Stipa tenacissima)* once used in the manufacture of fishing nets. Steps lead down to the photogenic cove, with its fishermen's cottages, boats, and restaurants. These include Chez Fonfon, famous for its *Bouillabaisse*, and Chez Jeannot, which has been serving good Pizza since 1949.

Continuing onwards, at Place Paul Ricard the Corniche turns inland. Pause to observe the gable-end mural of a coast guard and the Endoume headland with its blue-shuttered French Foreign Legion convalescent and retirement complex. Offshore is the Rocher des Pendus (Hangman's Rock), where in 1423, Alfonso V of Aragon (1396–1458) attempted to crush his rival to the throne of Naples, Louis III of Anjou (1403–1434), by hanging a dozen of his supporters.

The Corniche regains the coast at another stone viaduct built across the Anse de la Fausse Monnaie (Counterfeit Money Cove). Unfortunately the origin of this curious name is unknown. On the shore, the elegant Petit Nice hotel has been in the hands of the Passédat family since 1917 and is where American actor Gene Hackman stayed whilst filming *The French Connection II* (1975). Out to sea is the tiny fortified Degaby Island: inland is the open-air Théâtre Sylvain and renowned Le Rhul restaurant.

Next is the Maregraphe, a sea-level measuring device in operation since 1885. Directly opposite is the hilltop Villa Valmer built in 1865 for a wealthy oil-

Vallons des Auffes is a highlight of the Corniche Kennedy

seed merchant and currently being converted into a hotel (see no. 44). From here, a cast concrete bench runs continuously along the Corniche for the next 1.9 miles making it the longest bench in the world. The section used by spectators at the Olympic Sailing Games 2024 has been clad in mosaics by local artists.

One last place of interest is the Mémorial des Repatriés l'Hélice (1971). Created in the shape of a propeller blade by local sculptor César Baldaccini (1921–1998), it commemorates the French repatriates *(pieds-noirs)* who left Algeria in 1962 following that country's independence. The Corniche ends at the Parc Balnéaire du Prado, where it merges into the Promenade Georges Pompidou.

Other locations nearby: 13, 14, 15, 17

17 An Underwater Museum

Secteur I (7th Arrondissement), the Underwater Museum of Marseille (Musée Subaquatique de Marseille) offshore from Plage des Catalans (note: visitors should be proficient swimmers, suitably equipped, and accompanied by one or more other divers, guided tours by appointment www.musee-subaquatique.com)

There are more than a thousand museums in France but only one of them is located underwater! The Underwater Museum of Marseille (Musée Subaquatique de Marseille) lies 100 metres offshore from the popular Catalans Beach (Plage des Catalans) (7th). More a gallery than a museum, its purpose is to deploy the novel sight of underwater sculptures as a means of highlighting man's threat to marine biodiversity and the importance of environmental protection.

A concrete Poseidon in Marseille's Underwater Museum

It is no surprise that the museum's founder, Antony Lacanaud, has a passion for both art and the ocean. His inspiration to combine the two came from British sculptor Jason deCaires Taylor (b. 1974), who in 2009 opened the world's first underwater museum in Cancún, Mexico. Lacanaud, together with World Freediving Champion Morgan Bourc'his, marine engineer Thierry Dubourdieu-Rayrot, and a team of enthusiastic colleagues, followed suit and opened their own museum in 2021.

The museum consists of eleven sculptures by eleven different artists, each submerged at a depth of five metres.

They are made from pH-neutral concrete that does not poison the water but instead acts exactly like stone in attracting marine plants and animals. Even in the few years since the museum opened, the sculptures have been significantly colonised, creating an artificial reef in the process that is being monitored by scientists. At night the sculptures are illuminated by suspended globes containing bioluminescent bacteria fished up from a depth of over 8,000 feet.

The subject of the sculptures themselves is telling. They include Poseidon by Christophe Charbonnel, a polar bear by Michel Audiard, five sea nymphs by Evelyne Galinski, a fish by Mathias Souverbie, a free diver by Thierry Trives, an octopus by Floriane Lisowski, and a giant sea urchin by Daniel Zanca. Each has been created to highlight a different aspect of the sea and its connection to our well being. Who knew, for example, that 130,000 tonnes of wild octopus are consumed annually in Europe, which is already twice as much as a decade ago?

Access to the museum, which is open all hours, is free and power boats are banned in the area. Guided tours are available by appointment and the museum's links with schools and research institutes mean that it has a strong educational bias. It is to be hoped that the good done by the museum will see its initial 15-year licence renewed in 2036.

For those looking for real history in the waters around Marseille there are numerous wrecks, notably around the Riou Archipelago (see no. 20). They include: a Roman cargo ship of the 1st century BC off Grand Congloué, which in 1952 became the first archaeological dive made by scuba pioneer Jacques-Yves Cousteau (1910–1997); a rare 16th century wreck of a vessel near Jarre Island carrying ceramics from Fréjus; and the liner *Liban*, which sank in 1903 after a collision near Maïre Island. There are aircraft, too, including the Lockheed P-38 Lightning aircraft in which Antoine de Saint-Exupéry (1900–1944), author of *The Little Prince*, perished during the Second World War. Such wrecks combined with clear blue waters, reefs, and impressive drop-offs have made Marseille the diving capital of France. Indeed, as early as 1934 Marseille boasted a shop selling diving supplies, and in 1948 it saw the creation of one of the first diving organisations.

Other locations nearby: 13, 14, 15, 16

18 A Unique Seaside Garden

Secteur I (7th Arrondissement), the garden of the Villa Santa Lucia at 8 Montée de la Napoule (note: open Jul & Aug Sun–Wed 8am–2pm, rest of the year guided tours for a minimum of 10 people by appointment only tel. 0622655205, villasantalucia.mh@gmail.com; tickets with cash only)

Marseille should be better known for its green spaces since it offers over seven hundred hectares of public parks and gardens. Take, for example, the Parc du Vieux Moulin (10th), with its ruined watermills, powered between 1259 and 1952 by the Huveaune River. Or the Parc du 26ème Centenaire (also 10th), created to mark the city's twenty-six centuries of history, which contains four thematic gardens (Provencal, Oriental, African, and Asian) symbolising Marseille's cultural mix.

A garden unique in Marseille belongs to the Villa Santa Lucia in the Roucas Blanc neighbourhood (7th). The villa was built in 1860 at the top of a steep plot of land overlooking the Corniche Kennedy and the Plage du Prophète. The garden, which is laid out across seven terraces known in Provence as *restanques*, is entirely surrounded by a high stone wall. Access for visitors is either from above via Traverse Nicolas or from below by means of the 300-step Montée de la Napoule.

Between 1887 and 1905, the villa was occupied by the Mullot family. They enlarged the building and during the 1890s created a magical pleasure garden. Notably they commissioned the *faux* stalactite grottoes, wooden handrails, and bamboo belvedere all painstakingly constructed from cement moulded onto a wire frame. They are representative of the art of *rocaille* landscaping, which was in vogue in Marseille between 1870 and the Great War. In two places can be seen the signature of Gaspard Gardini, an Italian master of the technique, who worked in the garden between 1892 and 1894. Look out for his humorous touches, including a Pierrot peeping through a window and a soldier behind the battlements of a castle.

During the Mullot family's tenure, the villa was known as the Maison Blanche. The villa then changed hands many times until 1984, when it was acquired by the Renard family. By their time the property was known as the Villa Santa Lucia and it is they who share the garden with today's visitors. The family are rightly proud of the garden's organic and sustainable credentials.

Manmade structures aside, the garden's south-westerly aspect favours an impressive collection of Mediterranean and subtropical plants numbering more than two hundred species. These are the result of a major replanting in 1979, when exotic species were introduced by Parisian landscape gardener Tobie Loup de Vianne, to supplement the existing indigenous Stone or Umbrella Pines *(Pinus pinea)*. From 1984 onwards, owner Jean-Léopold Renard diligently restored the rockwork terraces and belvedere. For his efforts, in 2009 he received the Special Prize of the Prince Louis de Polignac Foundation in Paris.

A secret seaside garden at the Villa Santa Lucia

The garden's trees today include the columnar Mediterranean or Florence Cypress *(Cupressus sempervirens)* (sometimes called *Cyprès de Provence*), the Japanese Sago Cycad *(Cycas revoluta)*, the evergreen Tulip Laurel *(Magnolia grandiflora)*, and the humble European Olive *(Olea europaea)*. There are also citrus trees, including the thick-skinned Citron *(Citrus medica)* and its more common hybrid the Lemon *(Citrus x limon)*, the Bitter Orange *(Citrus x aurantium)*, the Bergamot Orange *(Citrus bergamia)*, and the Kumquat *(Citrus eufortunella)*. And there are various palm trees, too, including the South American Jelly Palm *(Butia odorata)*, the cold-hardy Mediterranean Dwarf Palm *(Chamaerops humilis)*, and the Date Palm *(Phoenix dactylifera)*.

The garden also features a collection of succulents, notably the spiky Century Plant *(Agave Americana)*, which is a staple of drought-tolerant gardens, the felty Elephant's Ear Kalanchoe *(Kalanchoe Beharensis)*, and various Aloes. The garden's inventory is rounded out with plants grown for their fragrance, namely mimosa *(Acacia dealbata)*, lavender, and lemon-scented geraniums.

Since 2020, the villa and garden have been jointly recognised by prefectural decree as an Historic Monument.

19 Monte Cristo's Prison

Secteur I (7th Arrondissement), the Château d'If on the island of If (Île d'If) (note: ferries depart daily from Embarcadère Frioul If at 1 Quai de la Fraternité (formerly Quai des Belges) but do not call at the island when the mistral is gusting)

A couple of miles west of Marseille's Old Port (Vieux Port) lies the Frioul Archipelago (Îles du Frioul) (see no. 20). The smallest and best known of its four islands is the former prison island of If (Île d'If). It was here that Edmond Dantès, the main protagonist in the novel *The Count of Monte Cristo (Le Comte de Monte Cristo)*, was incarcerated. Written by Alexandre Dumas (1802–1870) and published between 1844 and 1846, the book gave Marseille its first taste of widespread literary fame.

The island is essentially a low-lying rock, some seven acres in extent. During a visit in 1516, the French King Francis I (1494–1547) identified it as a strategically important location from which to defend Marseille from naval attack. Accordingly, between 1524 and 1531, the rock was artificially levelled through the construction of ramparts at the water's edge. At the island's highpoint a castle – the Château d'If – was constructed. A three-storey keep with a central courtyard, it measures 92 feet on each side, with a large gun tower on three of its corners.

Despite its sturdy appearance, the castle's main military worth was as a deterrent. The renowned military engineer Vauban (1633–1707) later deemed the castle badly built, so it is probably a good thing it never witnessed any real action. The nearest it came when Holy Roman Emperor Charles V (1500–1558) threatened to attack Marseille only to abandon his plan. The island's location and strong offshore currents made it far more effective as a prison, which it became during the 1580s. Reserved for political and religious detainees, its inmates included the renowned lover of the Duke of Orléans, Philippe of Lorraine (1643–1702), and over 3,500 Huguenots (French Calvinist Protestants). Another was Gaston Crémieux (1836–1871), a Marseille-based lawyer and journalist, who led a local version of the short-lived revolutionary Paris Commune.

As was common practice in those days, prisoners were treated differently according to their wealth and social standing. The poorest were quite literally placed at the bottom, confined twenty or more in windowless cells beneath the castle. By contrast, well-to-do inmates were given their own private cells *(pistoles)* above, with windows, fireplace, and privy *(garderobe)*.

The forbidding prison walls of the Château d'If

Of course, the island's most famous prisoner, Edmond Dantès, was fictional. A commoner who later purchases the noble title of count, he is wrongly imprisoned in the Château d'If for fourteen years. He then makes a daring escape becoming the first person ever to do so and to survive, a feat no real prisoner ever achieved.

In 1890, the island's use as a prison ended and it was demilitarized. Opened to the public immediately afterwards, its fame as the setting for Dumas' novel has guaranteed visitors ever since. Indeed, despite being uninhabited, it is one of the most frequented sites in all Marseille, with around 100,000 visitors annually. Some will no doubt have seen the island featured in the film *The French Connection* (1971). Despite claims to the contrary, however, there is no evidence that either the Marquis de Sade or the Man in the Iron Mask were ever here.

No less notorious than the Château d'If is Marseille's Baumettes Prison (9th). Opened in 1939, its walls have incarcerated murderers and crime bosses, resistance fighters and independence activists. Three of the last four executions in France were carried out here using a guillotine, the last in 1977. Remarkably Baumettes contains the country's only prison restaurant open to the public (www.lesbeauxmets-marseille.fr), which helps to train and socialise prisoners as they transition back into society.

Other locations nearby: 20

20 Boat Trip to the Islands

Lying off the coast of Marseille are twenty-three islands and islets. The Riou Archipelago off the southern coast consists of five islands (Maïre, Jarre, Jarron, Plane, and Riou) and six islets (Tiboulen de Maïre, Les Pharillons, Les Moyades, Les Impériaux, and Grand and Petit Congloué). A joy for scuba divers, it is the only uninhabited archipelago on the French continental coast. The Endoume Islands to the west consist of three islands (Endoume, Rocher des Pendus, and fortified Degaby), and the Îlot du Planier lighthouse on the far horizon stands in splendid isolation.

This leaves the Frioul Archipelago, which for a combination of wild nature, history and a sense of escape, takes some beating. Located just two miles from the Old Port (Vieux Port), and easily accessible by daily ferry, it consists of two main islands, Pomègues and Ratonneau, as well as the prison island of If, and five islets: Tiboulen de Ratonneau, Bermond, Eyglaudes, and Grand and Petit Salaman. Covering a total area of some 500 acres, and officially a part of the Calanques National Park (Parc National des Calanques), the archipelago is home to around 150 people (see no. 42).

A ferry entering the Old Port with Ratonneau island in the background

The ferry from the Old Port takes just 20 minutes to reach the Island of If. Despite being far smaller than Ratonneau and Pomègues, it receives many more visitors due to its connection with the famous novel *The Count of Monte Cristo* (see no. 19). From there it is only another 15 minutes' sailing time to reach the port on Ratonneau, where this adventure begins.

With its 700-berth marina and cluster of houses, shops, and cafés, Ratonneau's port bustles in the summer months. But just a short distance away there are winding paths that lead to secretive rocky coves *(calanques)*, abandoned gun emplacements, and two sizeable but disused forts. The largest, in the centre of the island, was built in 1886 and expanded by German forces during the 1940s, which explains the curious concrete crosses, which are in fact supports for an unfinished ammunition store.

Overlooking the marina is the eyecatching headquarters of Marseille's harbour pilots (Maison des Pilotes) built in 1947 in the shape of a ship's prow. Farther east and clearly signposted is the partially-ruined Caroline Hospital (Hôpital Caroline). This quarantine facility was built in the 1820s in anticipation of the arrival of foreign sailors with contagious yellow fever (fortunately it never reached Marseille). Named after Marie-Caroline, Duchess of Berry (1798–1870), the hospital was instead used to treat prisoners and those with infectious diseases, and was only abandoned in 1941. With restoration underway, including the neo-Classical chapel, it is hoped the hospital will eventually be opened to visitors. The small cliff-edge building on the way to the hospital is the Villa Marine, an information hub celebrating the biodiversity of the Frioul Archipelago.

A sea wall built in 1822 to form a port for the vessels of sailors in quarantine connects Ratonneau with Pomègues, which has a wilder, more rugged aspect. Like Ratonneau, however, its shoreline is indented with rocky coves, and it has various abandoned military installations, as well as a pair of old forts. A footpath running along its spine offers some breathtaking views. The plants, seabirds, and wind-sculpted rock formations add to the experience especially when the Mistral is gusting. Undoubtedly the best time to visit is between April and June, when the sun is not too hot, the wild flowers (including miniature iris) are blooming, and the noisy seagulls are nesting. Do not, however, attempt to approach them as they can be fiercely protective.

Other locations nearby: 19

Secteur II (2nd Arrondissement), the Museum of European and Mediterranean Civilisations (Musée des Civilisations de l'Europe et de la Méditerranée) (MuCEM) at 1 Esplanade du J4

Marseille as founded in 600 BC occupied three hills, which today form the neighbourhood of Le Panier. The westernmost hill, Saint-Laurent, was the original shoreline until the mid-19th century, when it was extended through landfill to create the Joliette Docks. Until 1988, when maritime activity relocated farther north, the southernmost Pier Number 4, which accommodated vessels plying the Marseille–Algiers route, was occupied by a large warehouse. Its demolition in 2009 created a vast space between the Cathedral and Fort Saint John. Known today as Esplanade du J4, it lies at the heart of a new cultural and business quarter called the Euroméditerranée Zone.

The completion of the Esplanade was timed to coincide with Marseille's crowning in 2013 as European Capital of Culture. It consisted of a public promenade named after influential local publisher Robert Laffont (1916–2010), the Museum of European and Mediterranean Civilisations (Musée des Civilisations de l'Europe et de la Méditerranée), and the Villa Méditerranée conference centre (now the Cosquer Méditerranée cave replica) (see no. 23). The showpiece project has since become a touch-

A gallery in the Museum of European and Mediterranean Civilisations (MuCEM)

stone for attracting new investment to facilitate Marseille's ongoing reinvention as a visitor destination.

The Museum of European and Mediterranean Civilisations (MuCEM) was the first French national museum to be located outside Paris. Dedicated to the cultural anthropology of European and Mediterranean societies, it occupies a landmark structure designed by Algerian-born architect Rudy Ricciotti (b. 1952). Occupying a perfectly square footprint, it is clad in concrete latticework that glows at night (see back cover). A greater part of the permanent collection was originally displayed in Paris as the National Museum of Popular Arts and Traditions (Musée National des Arts et Traditions Populaires). The current holdings encompass not only archaeology and anthropology but also modern history and contemporary art, from tools and trade signs to costumes and ceramics. In addition to permanent displays on the ground and second floors, ground-breaking temporary exhibitions are staged on the first floor. The MuCEM also encompasses the medieval Fort Saint John to which it is connected by a 427-foot-long aerial walkway, the Passerelle Fort Saint-Jean (see no. 13). A separate exhibition illustrates the history of the fort.

The Esplanade du J4 is only one part of the planned Euroméditerranée Zone, which will eventually encompass all four piers of the Joliette Docks stretching for a quarter of a mile. Pier 3 beneath the cathedral, for example, has been earmarked for an ecology hub scheduled to open in 2026, and the warehouse on Pier 1 built during the 1920s by the Eiffel Company will be reworked as a leisure complex. The docks' four vast late 19th century warehouses on Quai du Lazaret have already been adapted to house the Les Docks Village leisure and office complex. A little farther north are further relics of the docks, including the CEPAC silo (originally a sugar store and now serving as a concert hall) and the Dock des Sud at 12 Rue Urbain V (a former spice warehouse now used as an events' venue).

The Mediterranean theme is continued in the nearby Regards de Provence Museum (Musée Regards de Provence) on Avenue Vaudoyer. Housed inside a former Sanitary Station (Station Sanitaire) built in 1948 to control infection within the port, it contains around 850 Provençal works of art by the likes of Raoul Dufy (1877–1953), Félix Ziem (1821–1911), and Adolphe Monticelli (1824–1886). The landscape paintings are a reminder that although Marseille is known chiefly as a port, it also encompasses a vast rural hinterland.

Other locations nearby: 22, 23, 24, 28

22 The Nazi Round-Up

On Avenue Vaudoyer (2nd) at the foot of Fort Saint John (Fort Saint-Jean) there is a formidable concrete bunker. Completed in late-1943 as part of Hitler's Mediterranean Wall *(Südwall)*, its purpose was to provide medical support to the German Navy *(Kriegsmarine)* in the event of an Allied landing. Its purpose today, however, is very different. It houses the Deportations' Memorial (Mémorial des Deportations), which documents Nazi repression in Marseille between the arrival of German forces in November 1942 and their eviction in August 1944.

Through the documentation of individual lives, the memorial focuses on the Marseille Round-Up (Rafle de Marseille). This was the systematic removal of Jews, Communists, and resistance fighters from the densely-occupied Le Panier neighbourhood, which SS General Karl Oberg (1897–1965) branded "a hideout for international bandits" (as well as a refuge for German military deserters). It should be remembered that between June 1940 and November 1942 Marseille lay in the French Zone Libre (Free Zone) and so served as a haven for the opponents of Nazism. With the direct Occupation, the Vichy Regime, which administered Marseille, collaborated with the Germans and the haven was inevitably compromised.

The Round-Up (known officially as Operation Sultan) took place between the 22nd and 24th of January, 1943. Assisted by Vichy French police under the direction of René Bousquet (1909–1993), the SS led the raid into Le Panier. Simultaneously, Bousquet extended the operation into Marseille's 1st Arrondissement. Together, the two police forces checked the identity papers of 40,000 people. Of those, almost 6,000 were arrested, 20,000 were interned and their belongings expropriated, and 3,500 mainly Jews sent via Compiègne in the Northern Zone of France to the extermination camps. Others had already been apprehended and routinely tortured at Gestapo headquarters in a villa at 425 Rue Paradis (8th).

With the occupants of Le Panier removed, the neighbourhood and its once-popular red light district was levelled to make way for redevelopment. With the exception of just three historic buildings, which the Germans deemed worth saving, almost 2,000 tenement buildings were destroyed (see no. 26). This explains why visitors today will encounter

A Nazi-era bunker houses the Deportations' Memorial

so few old buildings between the Quai du Port and Rue Caisserie. Of the operation, the Nazi propaganda magazine *Signal* boasted that "In the future, when we shall write the history of Marseille, we will underline this remarkable feat that…had used French and German policemen". The event was later depicted in the British film *Seven Thunders* (1957) and is memorialised in front of the Hôtel Dieu in the form of an emaciated figure atop a granite plinth.

The eventual liberation of Marseille from the Nazis took place on the morning of 28th August, 1944. A key event was the capture of the Basilica of Notre-Dame de la Garde (Basilique Notre-Dame de la Garde) on 25th August by infantrymen supported by armoured tanks (heavy artillery and air raids were not options due to the historical importance of the site). A wall plaque at 26 Rue Jules-Moulet (6th) identifies a staircase unknown to the Germans, which enabled Algerian riflemen to access the hillside surrounding the church safely. They were supported by tanks from various directions, one of which was halted by the enemy on Place du Colonel Edon, where it is still parked today. By the evening, the hill had been retaken followed three days later by the liberation of the city. A declaration to that effect was made by Chairman of the Provisional Government, Charles De Gaulle (1890–1970), from the balcony of the Préfecture building on Place Félix Baret (6th).

Other locations nearby: 21, 23, 24, 25, 27

23 The Cosquer Cave Drawings

The Calanque de Morgiou is one of the many rocky inlets that define Marseille's jagged southern shore. In 1985, a professional diver from Cassis called Henri Cosquer (b. 1950) found something extraordinary here. Following a tip-off from a friend, he descended 121 feet to a submerged cave entrance. Inside he discovered an ascending gallery leading to an air pocket. It contained several hundred prehistoric cave drawings dating back as far as 34,000 BC.

Cosquer's discovery did not happen overnight though. Throughout 1985 he returned several times to Morgiou, each time venturing further into the gallery. Eventually, after penetrating 574 feet, he reached a point where the gallery abruptly turned upwards 90 degrees to open into the bottom of an underground lake. Unfortunately, a lamp failure forced his return, and it was not until 1990 that he returned with two Belgian cave divers, the brothers Bernard and Marc Van Espen. This time they were forced back by their guide line being too short.

Stencilled human hands at the Cosquer Méditerranée cave replica

In June 1991, Cosquer and Marc Van Espen returned to the cave and were able to explore briefly the air pocket above the lake. It took one further dive, on 9th July 1991, for Cosquer, his niece, and two friends from his local diving club to explore more thoroughly the air pocket. During this visit they saw the outline of a human hand on one of the walls. Further dives revealed the series of prehistoric drawings that are famous today.

Tragically, on 1st September 1991, three divers from Grenoble perished after losing their way in the submerged gallery. As a result, Cosquer made the cave's existence known to the Department of Maritime Affairs in Marseille. For the next fourteen years, the Cosquer Cave, as it became known, was the domain of professional prehistorians. They revealed how during the glacial periods of the Pleistocene, the geological epoch that lasted between c. 2.58 million and 11,700 years ago, the shore of the Mediterranean was several miles to the south. As a result, the sea level was as much as 330 feet below the entrance of the cave, which would have been high and dry. Only during the subsequent Holocene era did sea levels rise, drowning four-fifths of the cave and with it most of the drawings.

The almost five hundred drawings that do survive, however, are remarkable enough. They date from two distinct phases during the Upper Palaeolithic era. The first, from between 34,000 and 22,000 years ago, consists of 65 hand stencils (44 black and 21 red) undertaken by hunter-gatherers known as Gravettians. The second, from between 22,000 and 10,000 years ago, includes more complex animal and human figures by Epigravettians. These include horses, ibex, deer, bison, aurochs, and the curious Saiga antelope, as well as marine creatures such as penguins, seals, great auks, and even jellyfish. The penguins in particular illustrate how much colder the climate was when the drawings were made.

Today, the entrance to the Cosquer Cave is sealed to avoid further fatalities. Instead, since 2022 visitors have been able to experience a truly magnificent replica installed in the Villa Méditerranée on Promenade Robert Laffont/Esplanade du J4 (2nd) (the building boasts the world's longest inhabited cantilever at just over 131 feet). Here visitors can admire the drawings safely in self-driving cars, without getting their feet wet! Most will conclude that the replica cavern is every bit as impressive as the original. With a million visitors admitted within the first fifteen months, the Cosquer Cave replica has become one of Marseille's must-see attractions.

Other locations nearby: 21, 22, 24, 25, 27, 28

24 Cathedrals Old and New

Secteur II (2nd Arrondissement), Marseille Cathedral on Place Albert Londres

For more than fifteen centuries, Marseille Cathedral has occupied the same commanding position. Originally a sea-girt bluff in the north-west corner of the walled city, today it is a broad open terrace overlooking the manmade quayside of the Joliette Docks below.

The building is known officially as the Cathédrale Basilique Sainte-Marie-Majeure although locals prefer La Major for short. What makes it especially interesting is that the current building sits happily alongside the partially-ruined remains of its smaller predecessor. The old cathedral, or Vielle Major, was constructed from 381 AD onwards making it Marseille's oldest place of Christian worship. Clearly reworked numerous times, the most visible parts date from the 12th century. These comprise one bay of the original tripartite nave and the choir, which were spared when the present cathedral was built. When complete this was one of the finest Romanesque structures in Provence.

Inside there is a late-15th century terracotta bas-relief representing the descent from the Cross. It is attributed to the sculptor Luca della Robbia (1399–1482), who championed the use of colourful, tin-glazed terracotta statuary during the Renaissance period. It can also be noted that the French Baroque composer Charles Desmazures (1669–1736) was organist in the old cathedral. He dedicated his *Pièces de Simphonie* (1702) to Maria Luisa of Savoy (1688–1714) on her marriage to French-born Philip V of Spain (1683–1746).

The new cathedral is vast by comparison (see back cover). Indeed, with a length of almost 480 feet, a main cupola 230 feet high, and room for 3,000 worshippers, it ranks as one of the largest cathedrals in France. The foundation stone was laid by Emperor Napoleon III (1808–1873) in 1852, with the finished building eventually consecrated in 1897. The work of architect Léon Vaudoyer (1803–1872) and his pupil Henri-Jacques Espérandieu (1829–1874), it is rendered in a fusion of neo-Romanesque and neo-Byzantine styles. This is evidenced by the soaring arches and domes, and the eyecatching use of alternating horizontal bands of green Gonfolina sandstone and white Calissane limestone on the façade (the same device is used at the hilltop Basilica of Notre-Dame de la Garde by the same architects; see no. 38). Istanbul's Hagia Sophia Grand Mosque clearly provided inspiration in a deliberate effort to reflect Marseille's multicultural reputation.

The façade is further enlivened with statues of Christ, the Apostles, Saints Peter and Paul, and the Saints of Provence, with a bronze statue of Henri François Xavier de Belsunce (1671–1755) on the forecourt. Bishop of Marseille during the Great Plague of 1720, he is remembered for his tireless efforts to relieve the suffering of the people. During the Second World War, resistance fighters hid the statue in a warehouse to prevent the Germans melting it down.

Inside the cathedral, the architectural pattern continues, although the stone banding changes in colour to grey and orange. The sculptures, bronzework, and Venetian-style mosaics are the

Marseille's Old Cathedral with La Major in the background

work of Henri Révoil (1822–1900), who took over the project after the death of the original architects. With little expense spared, the materials used include white Carrara and Calissane marbles, Florentine green stone, limestone from the Gard, and even Tunisian onyx.

Designated a Basilica Minor by the Pope in 1896 for its historical and architectural value, the cathedral has been the seat of the Archdiocese of Marseille since its elevation in 1948.

Other locations nearby: 21, 22, 23, 25, 27, 28

25 A Stroll through Le Panier

Secteur II (2nd Arrondissement), a walk through the neighbourhood of Le Panier

All Marseille guidebooks point visitors in the direction of Le Panier. Little wonder since the unofficial neighbourhood is what most visitors seek in a city: a warren of narrow, car-free streets; gently-crumbling houses; boutique stores; and artisan cafés. What follows is one possible route through the area.

The tour begins on the Quai du Port, outside the flamboyant City Hall (Hôtel de Ville) of 1673. That it is the only old building on the waterfront reflects the fact that almost everything else between here and Rue Caisserie was destroyed in 1943 by the occupying Germans (see no. 26). Take Rue de la Mairie on the right and walk uphill to a broad open square. Here stands a memorial commemorating the Greek seafarers Euthymenes and Pytheas, both of whom lived in Massalia, as ancient Marseille was known. On the left are some chunky limestone footings from a Roman bath building completed in c. 50 AD. They are a reminder that the Panier Hill (Butte du Panier) represents the oldest part of Marseille, where the original Greek colony was founded in 600 BC (see no. 1).

Continue to the top and imagine staying in the magnificent Intercontinental Hotel Dieu on Place du Mazeau. Filling the skyline, this magnificent mid-18th century building was once a hospital (see no. 27). Turn left along Place Daviel and onto Rue Caisserie. On the right is the medieval Church of Notre-Dame-des-Accoules. Largely destroyed during the French Revolution for accommodating assemblies against the Convention, only its medieval bell tower is original.

A few steps ahead is Place des Augustines. It is named after an Augustinian order that once occupied the building at the top of the square, which now contains an atmospheric art gallery. The building at number 14 is where Napoleon Bonaparte spent two nights in February 1794, just prior to becoming artillery commander of the Army of Italy.

Continue onwards and turn right onto Rue Beauregard. A flight of steps leads upwards past graffitied walls to a narrow path lined with pot plants strung with inspiring quotations. Cross the street at the top, Montée des Accoules, and walk upwards along Rue des Moulins. The buildings on Place des Moulins escaped the destructions of the Second World War, although only three stumps remain of the seven-

The Hôtel de Ville and Notre-Dame-des-Accoules church are landmarks of Le Panier

teen 16th century windmills referenced in the name.

Exit the square at the far side, passing An Kamm's art studio on the left, to reach Rue du Panier and continue downhill. Why this street, and the area as a whole, is called 'Panier' is unclear. Meaning 'basket' in French it might have been an old inn sign, or as 'bread basket' perhaps it referenced the windmills used to grind wheat, or even the markets that were in the area in ancient times. Whatever the truth, today Rue du Panier buzzes with tourists.

Rue Rodillat on the right leads to the Vielle Charité and its museums (see no. 28). At the bottom of Rue du Panier, Rue de l'Évêché continues downhill into Place de Lenche, formerly the site of the ancient Greek agora; the later Roman forum was farther down on Rue Sainte-Laurent. This tour ends here with the partially-ruined Church of Sainte-Laurent. Marseille's only extant medieval church, it is now surrounded by 1950s housing. It has long been associated with the city's Neapolitan fishermen, whose descendants still carry a statue of the Virgin through the streets each Assumption Day (August 15th).

Other locations nearby: 22, 23, 24, 26, 27, 28

26 Fragments of Old Marseille

As with any great city, the heart of Marseille has altered enormously over the years. Buildings have been erected, demolished, and replaced, roads carved out and rerouted, and all manner of utilities installed. In many cases, what one sees today can only hint at what came before. There are rare occasions, however, when a structure survives down the centuries. Here are three of them.

The Maison Diamantée at 3 Rue de la Prison (2nd) stands just behind the City Hall. Commissioned sometime around 1570 by wealthy Italian and Spanish merchants, it is one of Marseille's oldest extant buildings. It owes its name to the eye-catching diamond-like plasterwork that covers much of the façade. Clearly designed to impress, the building was for a time home to the aristocratic Saboulin Bollena family, who were the first to organise maritime trade between Marseille and the West Indies. If the front door is open, sneak a peek at the magnificent staircase inside.

That the Maison Diamantée has survived intact for 450 years is remarkable. That it survived the events of February 1943 is nothing short of miraculous. It was in this month that the occupying Germans

The Maison Diamantée survived the destructions of World War Two

set about razing the neighbourhood of Le Panier, which they saw as harbouring resistance fighters, Jews, and Communists (see no. 22). Some 30,000 residents were expelled and almost 2,000 tenement buildings demolished. The Maison Diamantée was one of only three buildings spared for their historic value. The others were the Baroque City Hall (Hôtel de Ville) on the waterfront and the Hôtel de Cabre at 27 Grand Rue (see nos. 5, 25).

The Hôtel de Cabre is considered Marseille's oldest extant house having been built around 1535 for Consul Louis de Cabre, a local merchant and alderman (*échevin*). Its mix of Gothic and Renaissance building elements make it stand out today against the surrounding buildings. Effigies of de Cabre, his wife, and father still adorn the façade although the coat of arms with *fleur-de-lys*, a potent royal symbol, was removed by anti-monarchists during the French Revolution. In 1954, the building was threatened with demolition to make way for a redevelopment of the surrounding neighbourhood, which necessitated the widening of the Grand Rue. Rather than dismantling the building and rebuilding it elsewhere, however, it was moved bodily (all 670 tons of it!) on a railway from its original location on Rue Bonneterie to its current position fifty feet away, where it was rotated ninety degrees and lowered into place.

A third architectural fragment of old Marseille is situated away from Le Panier but was once connected with it. In Place Gilberto Bosques (2nd), opposite the Porte d'Aix, can be found a single remaining arch from the Huveaune Aqueduct. Dating from the 13th century, it once brought water from the Jarret, a tributary of the Huveaune, as far as Le Panier, watering some 380 city wells along the way. It continued to do this until 1849, when water from the Durance, a tributary of the Rhône, arrived via the newly-dug Canal de Marseille (see no. 33). Thereafter, the aqueduct was abandoned and largely demolished as it obstructed traffic and suburban development (and the Jarret was culverted). The course of the aqueduct has now largely been forgotten, although it probably ran along Rue Bernard du Bois to the east and and towards what is now Rue de la République in the west, passing through the old city ramparts along the way.

Other locations nearby: 1, 5, 8, 25, 27, 28

27 From Hospital to Hotel

Secteur II (2nd Arrondissement), the Intercontinental Hotel Dieu at 1 Place Daviel

There are currently just over a hundred hotels in Marseille. Ranging from modest to luxurious, they offer something for everyone, and some interesting history, too.

When it comes to extravagance, the 5-star Hôtel-Dieu at 1 Place Daviel (2nd) is hard to beat. Those fortunate enough to stay here, however, may be surprised to learn that the place was once a hospital (the name *Hôtel-Dieu* is an old French term for a hospital or almshouse). As a hospital, it was founded in the late-16th century by the merger of two existing hospitals, the Saint-Jacques de Galice and the Saint-Esprit. The latter had roots stretching back to 1188.

The present building, which dates from 1753, continued to accommodate patients right up until 1993, when it was used instead as a school for doctors and paramedics. Only in 2006 did it cease to serve a medical purpose, and in 2013 it was converted into a hotel. A branch of the InterContinental hotel group, it offers two Michelin-starred restaurants, one of which, the Brasserie Les Fenêtres, has a terrace with superb views of the Old Port (Vieux Port) and the hilltop Basilica of Notre-Dame de la Garde (see no. 38).

In front of the hotel are bronze busts of political caricaturist Honoré Daumier (1808–1879) and French ophthalmologist Jacques Daviel (1696–1762). Daviel was one of several volunteer medics who brought aid to Marseille during the Great Plague of 1720. He became surgeon-major at the city's Galley Arsenal (Arsenal des Galères), whilst also teaching at the Hôtel-Dieu. Oculist to King Louis XV (1715–1774), he is chiefly remembered for pioneering cataract extraction.

The Pavillon Daviel at 5 Rue de la Prison is also named in Daviel's honour. Once the city's courthouse (Palais de Justice), it was here during the French Revolution that sentences were handed down from the balcony, which overlooked a guillotine. In 1875, after the courthouse relocated to larger premises on Place Montyon (6th), it became Marseille's first public medical school, where theoretical courses were taught (clinical and anatomy courses were given at the Hôtel-Dieu). The school relocated to the Palais du Pharo in 1893 since when the building has served as an annexe to the town hall (see no. 14).

Down on the quayside are two more historic hotels. The Grand Hôtel Beauvau opened in 1816 and despite a revamp in 2016 it still radiates history. The Frédéric Chopin Suite recalls its most famous guest. Not far away is the Hôtel Belle-Vue, with its cosy first-floor Caravelle Bar and Restaurant, originally a cabaret venue for sailors in the 1920s.

Four blocks back from the Quai de Rive-Neuve is the Hotel C2, a smart boutique residence inside a 19th century townhouse. Alongside the frescoes and gilded ceilings are furnishings by Le Corbusier and Arne Jacobsen. The nearby Hotel Maison Montgrand occupies two similar townhouses and has the benefit of a shaded courtyard garden with its own *pétanque* court.

For seaside accommodation, Le Petit Nice Passedat at 17 Rue des Braves (7th) is a villa in the hands of the same family since 1917. The Tuba Club at 2 Boulevard Alexandre Delabre (8th) is an eco-friendly hotel and restaurant in an upcycled 1960s diving club once frequented by legendary free diver Jacques Mayol (1927–2001). The sea views from its five cabin-styled rooms are glorious.

The Intercontinental Hotel Dieu was once a hospital

A unique hotel in Marseille is the Chatterie Sainte-Cyle at 67 Rue de l'Audience (11th). Opened in 2013, this cattery offers individual and multiple-occupancy rooms depending on an individual cat's needs, as well as good food, company, and play.

Other locations nearby: 1, 5, 8, 25, 26, 28

28 The Old Charity

An architectural gem stands on the northern flank of the neighbourhood of Le Panier. The Vieille Charité at 2 Rue de la Charité (2nd) is a former 17th century shelter and workhouse for beggars. Surprisingly grand, with an oval Baroque chapel dedicated to Notre-Dame Mère de Charité (Our Lady Mother of Charity), it is almost entirely enclosed by a three-storey arcaded gallery. Today, as the Centre de la Vieille Charité, it hosts a variety of cultural institutions.

The Vieille Charité was designed by renowned painter, sculptor, and architect Pierre Puget (1620–1694). Born on nearby Rue du Petit Puis, his father a stonemason, Puget served his apprenticeship carving elaborate wooden ornaments for galleys in the Galley Arsenal (Arsenal des Galères) (see no. 9). From there he relocated to Italy, where he was greatly influenced by the Baroque. Upon his return to Marseille, he produced paintings for the city's Cathedral, and undertook several major municipal projects, notably laying out the Haussmann-esque Rue Canebière, Marseille's main central thoroughfare.

Work on the Vielle Charité began in 1671 and continued until 1745 due to financial restraints. Much of it is rendered in attractive pink and yellow sandstone hewn from the ancient quarries at Cap Couronne, twenty-five miles to the west. The latter part of the project, including the Baroque elliptically-domed chapel with Corinthian columns, was overseen by Puget's son, Françoise.

Beggars during the 17th century were treated harshly. Special guards called *Chasse-gueux* (Beggar Hunters) were employed to round them up. Non-residents were expelled, whilst natives were placed in workhouses in accordance with a Royal Edict of 1640. These included the Vieille Charité, where over a thousand beggars were registered in 1760. The lack of outward-looking windows in the building was so as not to offend passers-by with scenes of poverty.

By 1781, when containment of the poor became less acceptable, the number of residents had fallen to 250. The building subsequently served as an asylum for vagrants, a barracks for the French Foreign Legion, and lodgings for those rendered homeless by the destruction of the neighbourhood of Le Panier during the Second World War (see no. 22). Before its eventual renovation in 1986, the increasingly dilapidated building was home to 146 families attended by the Little Sisters of Jesus, as well as an

A Baroque chapel sits at the heart of the Vieille Charité

anchovy packing plant! The campaign to save the building from demolition was spearheaded by the architect, Le Corbusier.

As the Centre de la Vieille Charité, the building today is home to two permanent museums, a centre for poetry, various research facilities, and a temporary exhibition space. The Museum of Mediterranean Archaeology (Musée d'archéologie Méditerranéenne) on the first floor contains the second largest collection of ancient Egyptian artefacts after the Louvre, as well as material pertaining to Marseille's ancient Greek founders and the local Celto-Ligurian peoples before them (see no. 47).

The Museum of Africa, Oceanic and Native American Art (Musée d'Arts Africains, Océaniens et Amérindiens) on the second floor contains masks from West and Central Africa, decorated human skulls and dance masks from Oceania, and feather ornaments from Mexico. The International Poetry Centre (Centre International de la Poésie) on the ground floor is dedicated to the creation and dissemination of contemporary poetry.

The architect Pierre Puget is further memorialised by the Jardin de la Colline Puget at the top of Cours Pierre Puget (13th). Opened in 1801, it is Marseille's oldest public garden. Puget's bust stands at the entrance. If it's a hot day, walk back along Cours Pierre Puget to Station Uvale at number 27, where fresh-pressed grape juice *(Jus de Raisin)* has been sold since the 1940s.

Other locations nearby: 23, 24, 25, 26, 27

29 Art at the FRAC

Secteur II (2nd Arrondissement), the FRAC Sud–Cité de l'Art Contemporain at 20 Boulevard de Dunkerque

In 2013, Marseille was crowned European Capital of Culture. As part of the citywide celebrations, a new arts' centre was inaugurated in the burgeoning Euroméditerranée Zone cultural and business quarter. The holdings of the so-called FRAC Sud–Cité de l'Art Contemporain at 20 Boulevard de Dunkerque (2nd), as well as the audacious building in which they are displayed, have become a 'must see' for those interested in contemporary art and architecture. Visiting on foot takes in not only the ambitious new-builds in the area but also various converted old port warehouses.

The Provence-Alpes-Côtes d'Azur Regional Contemporary Art Fund (Fonds Régionaux d'Art Contemporain), or FRAC for short, was established in 1982 at the initiative of the Ministry of Culture. Founded on the basis of a State-Regions partnership, its designated goal is to encourage artistic creation, to support regional cultural planning, and to raise public awareness through exhibitions, thereby forging links between the region's contemporary artists and their public.

For thirty years, the FRAC was based in Le Panier. Then, in 2007, a

The façade of the FRAC Sud evokes fish scales

group of regional officials, state representatives, and art professionals met to discuss its relocation. They chose the Japanese architect Kengo Kuma (b. 1954) to design a new building in La Joliette. Kuma's stated goals as an architect are threefold: to adapt the minimalist tradition of Japanese architecture for the 21st century; to ensure that a building respects rather than dominates its neighbours; and to manipulate natural light through a building's construction materials. All three goals are achieved in the FRAC Sud–Cité de l'Art Contemporain.

Kuma's building consists of a main body connected by footbridges to a tower, which is cantilevered over a broad terrace. The façades are neatly clad with 1,700 enamelled glass panes that give the impression of fish scales or fabric. Each pane is hung at a particular angle to create a sense of interplay between the building and its surroundings. In this way the building sits comfortably with the surrounding modern structures and really comes alive.

The building's interior is influenced by Le Corbusier's Unité d'Habitation (1952) (see no. 43). Visitors wander freely through voluminous spaces that offer versatile exhibition opportunities subtly opened to the outside. The sixty thousand square feet of floor offers ample space to display more than a thousand works by some 540 international artists. For architect Kuma, it is a space designed specifically for works in a state of continuous flux and ever-changing public interaction. The result is an experimental art laboratory, offering around fifteen collective and thematic exhibitions annually, as well as events, meetings with artists, and workshops for all ages.

Fans of contemporary art might also care to visit the Musée d'Art Contemporain (MAC) at 69 Avenue D'Haïfa (8th). Showcasing French and international artists from the 1960s onwards, its permanent collection includes works by Buren, Christo, Niki de Saint Phalle, Tinguely, and Warhol, and local artists such as Ben and César. Some works are displayed in the garden.

Contemporary art in Marseille also inhabits more humble locations. Take, for example, the Southway Pavilion located not far from the MAC, at 433 Boulevard Michelet (9th). This hybrid studio, exhibition space, and artist's residency helps promote contemporary art away from the city centre. Les Ateliers Blancarde, a community library and resource centre on the first floor of the Blancarde SNCF station (4th), does the same. A so-called 'Third Place' location (neither home nor work), it forges social and cultural ties through the free circulation of artistic ideas and materials, and also hosts creative residencies.

Other locations nearby: 24, 28, 30

30 Towering Statistics

Marseille's first significantly tall structures were the Îlot du Planier Lighthouse (1881) at 194 feet and the Les Réformés Church (1886) and Cathedral (1893), which both clocked in at 230 feet (see no. 24). These were exceded in 1905 by the Transporter Bridge (Pont Transbordeur). The work of French engineer Ferdinand Joseph Arnodin (1845–1924), it consisted of four steel latticework pylons straddling the mouth of the Old Port (Vieux Port), each just over 280 feet high. The pylons were connected by a high-level railway beneath which a carriage was suspended on cables. This was used to transport people and goods to and fro across the water. Unfortunately, this impressive feat of engineering was destroyed at the end of the Second World War.

Marseille's first real tower block was Le Corbusier's Unité d'Habitation (1952) (see no. 43). Its seventeen residential floors, however, reaching only 184 feet, fell far short of the non-residential structures that had gone before. Subsequent towers improved on this but it was only during the 1960s that one finally exceeded the height reached by the Transporter Bridge. This was the 30-storey Building A of the sprawling La Rouvière housing complex (1968), which reached 312 feet and had a swimming pool on the roof.

The 1970s saw the record broken again with the construction of the Grand Pavois (1975). At 335 feet in height, it is currently Marseille's tallest residential building. It is only exceeded by Marseille's two tallest office blocks. The red-white-and-blue La Marseillaise Tower (2018) is the work of renowned French architect Jean Nouvel (b. 1945). An impressive 446 feet in height, it reached second place in the Emporis Skyscraper Awards 2018.

Standing nearby is the tallest office block in Marseille and the city's tallest building overall. Completed in 2010, it is the CMA CGM Tower (Tour CMA CGM) at 4 Quai d'Arenc (2nd), which tops out at 482 feet. The location is significant since the tower acts as a beacon for the Euroméditerranée Zone cultural and business district, which was conceived in 1995. Designed by the Iraqi architect Zaha Hadid (1950–2016) in her signature Deconstructivist style, the tower is headquarters to the Compagnie Maritime d'Affrètement–Compagnie Générale Maritime, the world's third largest shipping company. At the request of the then mayor, Jean-Claude Gaudin (1939–2024), the height of the tower did not exceed that of the hilltop Basilica of Notre-Dame de la Garde, the city's icon since its construction in 1864 (see no. 38).

Although the tower only ranks twenty-seventh in the list of the tallest structures in France, its statistics are still worth detailing: thirty-three floors; thirteen elevators; five underground parking levels; an 800-seat company restaurant; dedicated tram and rail stations; and a price tag of 300 million Euros.

The CMA CGM Tower is the tallest building in Marseille

There are some interesting artworks in the tower, too, including two large gold lacquer panels by Jean Dunand (1877–1942) in the large council room on the 31st floor. They originally decorated the First-Class smoking room of the French luxury liner *Normandie*. In front of the building, the monumental bronze *Le Génie de la Mer* by sculptor Carlo Sarrabezolles (1888–1971) was also intended for the liner but ended up being too heavy.

Not so far away at 7 Quai de la Joliette is the striking *Art Deco* former headquarters of the Compagnie Générale Transatlantique. State-founded in 1855 to ensure postal deliveries to North America, it built the *Normandie* and several other luxury French liners. In 1996, a merger saw it become part of the CMA CGM.

Other locations nearby: 29

31 A Tobacco Factory Transformed

Secteur II (3rd Arrondissement), the Friche la Belle de Mai at 41 Rue Jobin

Adaptive reuse is the art of repurposing old buildings. Marseille's maritime and manufacturing past has provided the city with a wealth of structures ripe for such conversion. Examples include a theatre in a former fish market hall, a hotel in what once was a hospital, and a sugar silo that is now a concert hall (see nos. 8, 21, 27). Most unusual is the huge Nazi-era submarine base codenamed 'Martha' at Terminal Cap Janet (15th) that has been converted into a secure data centre.

Another successful example is the Friche la Belle de Mai. This huge multipurpose arts' space is located inside a former 19th century tobacco factory. During the 17th century, the French state established a monopoly on the manufacture and sale of tobacco products. In Marseille, which was one of the main ports of entry for tobacco leaves, with a climate conducive to their drying, a cigar factory was opened near the Old Port (Vieux Port) at the corner of Rue Vacon and Rue Paradis (1st).

With the French Revolution, the state monopoly was abolished, only to be re-established during the First Empire. In 1868, with demand increasing, a much larger factory was opened in the Belle de Mai neighbourhood. With 1,250 workers, most of whom were women, it represented the largest concentration of female workers in the city. In 1873, the factory began producing cigarettes, which quickly overtook cigar sales. The creation in 1935 of the state-owned Tobacco and Matches Industrial Exploitation Service (Service d'Exploitation Industrielle des Tabacs et Allumettes) gave rise to the factory's acronymic name, SEITA.

By 1947, the entire manufacturing process – drying, shredding, rolling, and packing – was mechanised and the workforce reduced. The 1970s brought foreign competition and the anti-smoking lobby, so it was decided in 1985 to relocate the factory away from Marseille. This left the abandoned factory and its surroundings a wasteland, nicknamed the Friche la Belle de Mai (Belle de Mai Wasteland), which was ripe for reuse. The nickname stuck when it was decided to reinvent the factory as the cultural heart of a reinvigorated working-class neighbourhood. It should be remembered that at the time Marseille had one of the smallest cultural budgets, with no

The Friche la Belle de Mai is a factory turned arts and leisure centre

large-scale projects in the pipeline. The Friche la Belle de Mai project helped get Marseille back on track.

With almost half a million square feet of floor space, spread across three separate buildings, it is an exciting place to be. The Friche itself occupies the factory's former stores and brings all the arts under one roof. It includes six concert halls and and two performance spaces for music, theatre and dance, including a basement night club, as well as a skatepark, restaurant, bookshop, and rooftop terrace, with deckchairs and exhibition space. The factory's former manufacturing building now contains the Media Centre film studios and various professional spaces. The third building, the former administration building, is home to several highbrow cultural institutions, including the MuCEM Resource Conservation Centre, Goethe Institute Marseille, and Marseille Municipal Archives. Outside, parents bring their children to the play areas, whilst others spend time in the communal vegetable garden. There is plenty of space for street art, too.

Immediately south of the Friche is the Bénédit-Jobin road tunnel, which runs beneath the railway to reach the Longchamp neighbourhood. The otherwise gloomy space has been enlivened with 460 panels painted by Marseille-based artist Frédéric Clavière.

Other locations nearby: 32, 33

32 The Comet Chasers

Most visitors will be unaware of the importance Marseille has to play in the history of astronomy. As early as the 17th century, one Father Louis Feuillée (1660–1732) was making astronomical observations in the city. Two easy-to-find locations tell the rest of the story.

The first is the slightly scruffy-looking school building at 29 Montée des Accoules (2nd), a back street towards the top of the neighbourhood of Le Panier. Dating back to 1702, it was built by the Jesuits, the proselytizing Catholic order that placed such emphasis on education. The school contained an astronomical observatory, where the mathematician Joseph-Louis Lagrange (1736–1813) observed the 1761 Transit of Venus, and where the astronomer Jean-Félix Adolphe Gambart (1800–1836) identified thirteen comets.

The man most associated with the observatory, however, was not initially an astronomer at all. Jean-Louis Pons (1761–1831) was born into a poor family in the French Alps, where he received little formal eduction. He began working at the observatory as a humble doorman and caretaker. Despite this, he displayed a natural aptitude for astronomy, assisting the professionals with their observations. He was eventually able to make his own observations, exhibiting a remarkable ability to memorise star fields and the changes within them.

Pons spotted his first comet on 11th July, 1801 using a telescope of his own design. Nicknamed the *Grand Chercheur* (Great Seeker), it had a large aperture and short focal length much like later Comet Seeker telescopes. Although Pons was not especially detailed in recording his observations, he is credited with spotting thirty-seven comets between 1801 and 1827, which remains a record for the greatest number of comets discovered by one person. Several of them, including 7P/Pons–Winnecke, 12P/Pons–Brooks, and 273P/Pons–Gambart, bear his name. In 1813, Pons was made Assistant Astronomer at the observatory, where he remained until 1819, when he relocated to Italy. His achievements in Marseille are not forgotten though as witnessed by the wall plaque outside the school entrance today.

With light polution an increasing problem, the old observatory closed in 1863 (the building today contains the Préau des Accoules Children's Museum). On the advice of Urbain Le Verrier (1811–

1877), director of the Paris Observatory, a second observatory opened a year later farther out of the city. Accessible from Allée Jean-Louis Pons (4th), it occupies the same plateau as the Palais Longchamp (see no. 33). Of the various telescopes installed here, the most famous is a huge wooden 31.5 inch (80 cm) reflecting telescope designed by Léon Foucault (1819–1868) of Foucault's Pendulum fame. Instead of the usual polished bronze or tin reflectors, he used a parabolic silvered glass mirror. This was ten times more accurate than its predecessors and was used to discover hundreds of new nebulae. The largest telescope of its type when installed in 1865, it remained in use until its retirement a century later.

Léon Foucault's wooden telescope in Marseille's Historic Observatory

By this time, the activities of the new observatory had been supplemented by those of the Haute-Provence Observatory, opened in 1937 on a far higher plateau sixty miles north of Marseille. In 2008, the observatory's astrophysics' laboratory relocated to a new-build facility, the Technopôle Chateau-Gombert (13th), which also boasts Europe's first solar-powered restaurant! With observations now conducted elsewhere, the observatory on Allée Jean-Louis Pons has become the Marseille Historic Observatory (Observatoire Historique de Marseille), a museum and educational facility in which the Foucault telescope takes pride of place. Administered by the Andromede Association, an added attraction is a 30-seat planetarium installed in 2001.

Other locations nearby: 31, 33

33 Surprises at Palais Longchamp

One of Marseille's more unusual architectural ensembles is the Palais Longchamp. Commissioned by Emperor Napoleon III (1808–1873) on a platcau at the head of Boulevard Longchamp, the vast 19th century edifice is not a palace at all since no-one ever lived there. Instead, it stands as a monument to the opening in 1849 of the fifty-mile-long Canal de Marseille, which still supplies Marseille with two thirds of its drinking water.

Marseille originally drew its water from the Huveaune River, which was canalised in the 14th century. In time its flow became polluted and inadequate. The situation became chronic during the 1830s, when Marseille's rapid population growth was accompanied by droughts and a cholera epidemic. As a result of angry public protests, it was decided to bring in a more reliable supply of water from the nearest large river, the Durance.

Construction of the gravity-fed canal between the Durance and Saint-Antoine (15th), the highest point in Marseille, took fifteen years. It necessitated the construction of sixteen aqueducts and forty-one tunnels, and then a further forty-eight miles of distribution pipes,

A celebration of water at the Palais Longchamp

tanks, and basins within the city. In 1876, it was reported that the citizens of Marseille had over thirty times more water per person than they did before the canal opened. No wonder they felt like celebrating.

Although the foundation stone of the palace was laid in 1839, it took another thirty years to complete. It was designed by Henri-Jacques Espérandieu (1829–1874), who was also responsible for Marseille Cathedral and the Basilica of Notre-Dame de la Garde (see nos. 24, 38). The building essentially consists of three parts. In the centre is a magnificent pavilion called the Château d'Eau, which marks the terminus of the canal. In front there is a sculptural group by Pierre-Jules Cavelier (1814–1894) comprising four large Camargue bulls (symbolising the power of water) and three women. The central woman represents the Durance River, whilst the two others represent the vine and wheat, both symbols of fertility and abundance. Water flows out from beneath these figures down through a series of decorative pools and waterfalls.

Either side of the pavilion are semi-circular colonnades that terminate in a pair of large, self-contained wings. The north wing houses the Museum of Fine Arts (Musée des Beaux-Arts), which contains works by several Marseille-based painters, including Maurice Bompard (1857–1936), Joseph Garibaldi (1863–1941), Émile Loubon (1809–1863), and Alphonse Moutte (1840–1913). Founded originally in 1801 together with the School of Fine Arts in the Couvent des Bernardines, it is Marseille's oldest museum (the school ended up in the Palais des Arts on Place Carli (6th), also the work of Espérandieu).

The south wing contains the Natural History Museum (Musée d'Histoire Naturelle), with stuffed animals, fossils, and Neolithic remains from the Loubière Cave (13th). Some of the animals once lived in the zoo that was in the park behind the palace. Opened in 1854, it was the country's first provincial zoo. Financial woes, however, forced its closure in 1987 since when the cages and enclosures have stood empty, including the Oriental-style giraffe and elephant pavilions.

Both museums feature magnificent staircase frescoes on topical themes by the artists Jean Francis Auburtin (1866–1930) and Pierre Puvis de Chavannes (1824–1898).

Not far from the palace, at 140 Boulevard Longchamp, is the Grobet-Labadié Museum. This elegant mid-19th century townhouse is furnished with *objets d'art* indicative of the tastes of Marseille's affluent merchant class at its most successful. Closed at the time of writing, it can only be viewed from the outside.

Other locations nearby: 31, 32

34 How Pastis is Made

There is wine aplenty in Marseille, with nearby regions such as Bandol and Cassis boasting their own *appellations*. It is not wine, however, that first comes to mind when imbibing in the city. That honour goes to *pastis*, the potent aniseed-flavoured spirit that has become Marseille's signature *apéritif*.

There is a venerable Mediterranean tradition of aniseed spirits that includes Greek *ouzo*, Turkish *raki*, Italian *Sambuca*, and Lebanese *Arak*. The story of *pastis*, however, only goes back to 1915, when the French government outlawed drinks containing more than 16% alcohol for fear they were undermining the war effort. This included *Absinthe*, the notorious spirit made from wormwood *(Artemisia absinthium)* with its minimum alcohol content of 45%. As a result of the ban, the Marseillais began concocting their own aniseed-based spirit, which they called *pastis*, a word derived from either the French *pastiche* (meaning a stylistic imitation) or the Provençal word *pastís* (meaning a rough mixture).

During the 1920s, this home-made *pastis* famously caught the attention of Paul Ricard (1909–1997), the son of a Marseille wine merchant. He refined the drink with anise seeds *(Pimpinella anisum)*, star anise *(Illicium verum)*, liquorice root *(Glycyrrhiza glabra)*, and fennel seeds *(Foeniculum vulgare)*. The finished product was successfully trialled in the bars of Marseille and in 1932 the Ricard Company went into production. By 1938, sales of Ricard *pastis* topped 2.4 million litres and despite a ban during the Second World War, the company continued to expand. In 1975, Ricard merged with its main competitor, Pernod Fils, creating the Pernod Ricard group, which in 1984 produced its billionth bottle. Today it has factories across France.

A *pastis* brand that has remained loyal to Marseille is Cristal Limiñana at 99–101 Boulevard Jeanne d'Arc (5th). This company was founded in 1884 in Alicante to produce an aniseed-flavoured drink called *Paloma*. In 1897, the company relocated to Algeria, then a French colony, and in 1962, when Algeria gained independence, to Marseille. Fascinating factory tours led by the founder's great-granddaughter, Maristella Vasserot, reveal the processes that go into the making of their *pastis*. Firstly, an organic flavouring compound known as an anethole essence is created by the distillation of anise seeds and star anise. Secondly, macerated liquorice root is steeped in neutral 45% alcohol. The two are then blended with sugar (11 grams per litre) together with caramel, which imparts the distinctive yellow colour hence the alternative name *jaune*. The finished *pastis* is then bottled and stored above 12°C away from sunlight, to prevent the anethole from crystallising and impairing the flavour.

Bottles of pastis in the Cristal Limiñana factory shop

A well-stocked shop awaits visitors at the end of the tour. Here a dozen different aniseed spirits are available to purchase, including the company's signature *Pastis de Marseille* in its characteristic green bottle, and *Cristal Anis* in a clear hexagonal bottle. The latter is produced in a similar manner to *pastis* but is left colourless and has significantly higher sugar content. A liqueur rather than a spirit, it is called *anisette* or simply *anis*.

It is worth noting that *pastis* is best served cold in a 1-to-5 dilution with chilled water (ice cubes should only ever be added afterwards). Dilution releases the aroma of the aniseed and causes the *pastis* to turn milky. Such sage advice is on offer at La Maison du Pastis, a family-run shop at 108 Quai du Port (2nd). They offer almost a hundred different *pastises* and *absinthes*, including homemade concoctions decanted from metal barrels into customers' takeaway bottles.

Other locations nearby: 45

35 Graffiti Then and Now

Secteur IV (6th Arrondissement), street art on Rue Jean-Baptiste-Estelle and Cours Julien

Graffiti is defined as art that is written, drawn, or painted on a wall or other surface, usually without permission and within public view. It ranges from simple written monikers to elaborate murals, and has existed since prehistoric times. Marseille is unusual in that it has graffiti spanning several millennia.

The oldest graffiti – a word derived from the Greek γράφειν meaning 'to write' – takes the form of prehistoric cave art. In the early 1990s, a cave filled with figurative paintings was discovered in the Calanque de Morgiou, one of the many rocky inlets that define Marseille's jagged southern shore. Dating back 27,000 years, they include hand stencils and numerous animals (see no. 23).

The oldest written graffiti comes from ancient Greece and Rome, and consists of political comment, amorous declarations, and advertisements. Napoleon's soldiers carved their names on ancient monuments, a habit continued by American soldiers during the Second World War. Finally, during the 1960s and 70s, young Americans began spraying graffiti in the subways of New York City and Philadelphia. Fuelled by hip hop culture, the spray graffiti culture went global from there.

In Marseille, modern graffiti encompasses everything from simple "I was here" monikers and gang turf tags to large-scale message murals, and even works created from different materials. Examples can be found across the city, with worthwhile concentrations in the neighbourhood of Le Panier and the Friche de la Belle de Mai cultural venue (see no. 31 & back cover). The unquestioned epicentre of Marseille graffiti, however, is the Cours Julien (6th). Part of Notre-Dame du Mont, a neighbourhood occupying one of Marseille's seven hills, it was here that the city's wholesale fruit and vegetable market was located between 1860 and 1972, when it was abandoned in favour of the Arnavaux neighbourhood (14th). Later, during the 1990s, Cours Julien was discovered by graffiti artists and has since become the city's liveliest (and according to Time Out coolest) neighbourhood.

A stone's throw from the vibrant Maghrebi market on Place du Marché des Capucins, 'Cours Ju' is reached by a footbridge and staircase that lead from Rue d'Aubagne up Rue Jean-Baptiste-Estelle. Every inch of reachable wall and floor space is covered with graffiti making this one of the city's most photographed spots. Of particular interest is the corner of the right-hand building at the top of the stairs. A timeline of modern street art it encompasses traditional examples, including a niched Madonna and a blue-and-white street sign, and contemporary forms such as posters and spray-painted names. In amongst these are examples of street art made from different materials. Can you spot the terra-cotta monkey's face? And the small blue mosaic depicting a 1980s *Space Invaders* motif? The latter is the trademark work of Marseille-based street artist Invader, who works out of a studio on the roof of Le Corbusier's Unité d'Habitation apartment block (see no. 43). His mini-mosaics can be seen across Marseille, and in many other cities, too.

All sorts of street art on Rue Jean-Baptiste-Estelle

Cours Julien, with its artists and musicians, bars and pavement cafés, provides a canvas for more graffiti and myriad bars and art spaces. Continue northwards to pick up Rue Armand Bédarride on the left, which descends back down to Cours Lieutaud by means of another graffiti-covered staircase.

Street art in its broadest sense is undertaken at La Cité des Arts de la Rue at 225 Avenue Ibrahim Ali (15th). Located in a converted soap factory in the Les Aygalades neighbourhood, it can be identified by an upended bus at the entrance. The Aygalades Waterfall is within easy walking distance.

Other locations nearby: 45

36 The Cantini Fountain

Secteur IV (6th arrondissement), the Cantini Fountain on Place Castellane

The Rue de Rome, which straddles the 1st and 6th Arrondissements, is part of Marseille's central north–south axis. It was commissioned by King Louis XIV (1638–1715), who despite his personal extravagance did much to modernise France. In conjunction with Cours Belsunce and Rue d'Aix, the purpose of the Rue de Rome was to align the Porte d'Aix in the north with the Porte de Rome in the south, two monumental gateways through the city's former ramparts. Beyond the Porte de Rome, the road ran south as far as what is now Place Castellane, and during the 19th century was further extended along the Avenue du Prado, Marseille's most impressive thoroughfare.

Place Castellane today is an important roundabout handling two Metro lines and a tram terminus. A recent makeover has made it a pleasant place to muse further on its history. Back in the 18th century, the land hereabouts belonged to the aristocratic land owner and naval officer, Marquis Henri-César de Castellane-Majastre (1733–1789). In 1774, he donated the land to the City, with the proviso that it be suitably developed. Sadly, he did not live to see a fountain and wash house built on the square in 1798.

Later, in 1811, these features were joined by an obelisk erected to mark the birth of the doomed son of Emperor Napoleon I (1769–1821), as mentioned by Joseph Conrad in his 1919 novel *The Arrow of Gold*. In 1882, electric lighting was trialled on Place Castellane before being extended six years later along La Canebière. The obelisk remained in place until 1911, when it was relocated to the southern neighbourhood of Mazargues (9th).

The monumental fountain standing on Place Castellane today dates from 1913. It was financed by local sculptor and philanthropist Jules Cantini (1826–1916), hence it being called the Cantini Fountain. Son of an Italian sculptor, Cantini's work in Marseille consists mainly of church altars, which can be seen in the Cathedral (2nd), Les Réformés on Cours Franklin Roosevelt (1st), and the Church of Saint Joseph at 126 Rue Paradis (6th). He did not, however, create his namesake fountain, which is the work of Toulon sculptor André-Joseph Allar (1845–1926). Formed from Carrara marble and standing some eighty-two feet high, it consists of a column topped with a figure representing Marseille and, at its base, the stages of the River Rhône from source to

Sculptures at the base of the Cantini Fountain

sea. During the fountain's unveiling ceremony, the Mayor of Marseille flattered Cantini by comparing his generosity to that of Crinas, the 1st-century physician, who bequeathed ten million sesterces for the maintenance of ancient Marseille's fortifications.

A stroll around the perimeter of Place Castellane reveals a couple of elegant cafés, the abandoned Cinema Le César, two memorial plaques to fallen members of the French Resistance (F.F.I.), and a vintage-style cast-iron sales' kiosk.

Marseille has further tributes to Jules Cantini. Avenue Jules Cantini (6th) is named in his honour, as is the Musée Cantini, which occupies his former 17th century mansion at 19 Rue Grignan (6th). He stipulated in his will that it be used as an art museum, which opened in 1936. Initially, the collection focused on Provençal painters such as Maurice Bompard, Jean-Antoine Constantin, Adolphe Monticelli, and Gustave Ricard. Since then, its scope has broadened to encompass 20th century works by Antonin Artaud, Jean Arp, Francis Bacon, Balthus, Alberto Giacometti, Oskar Kokoschka, Henri Matisse, and Pablo Picasso. Another work by Cantini himself is a marble replica of Michelangelo's *David*, which stands on a roundabout near the Plages du Prado (8th). Carved in 1903, *Le David*, as it is known locally, appeared here in the 1950s.

Other locations nearby: 37

37 The Jews of Marseille

Secteur IV (6th Arrondissement), the Great Synagogue of Marseille (Grande Synagogue de Marseille) at 117 Rue Breteuil (note: visitors welcome with a form of identity and security check; men to wear a *kippah*)

As well as attracting merchants and economic migrants, Marseille has for centuries served as a safe haven for refugees. From Armenians escaping the Ottoman genocide to French repatriates returning from a newly-independent Algeria *(pied-noirs)*, each has brought something unique to an already cosmopolitan city. One community that sought both commercial gain and religious freedom is the city's Jews.

Jews have lived in Marseille since at least the 6th century AD, when they acted as trading intermediaries between Roman Gaul and the Levant. Their number grew in 576, when Jews arrived from Clermont to escape forced conversion to Christianity. Until 1040, they lived outside the city walls.

By the 12th century, around 300 Jews resided in Marseille in two distinct communities: spice merchants around the Old Port (Vieux Port) and Talmudic scholars *(yeshivot)* inland. Despite being granted citizen status in 1257, they remained subject to restrictions. These were only lifted by the tolerant Angevins during the 14th century, when the two communities became one and the Jews were integrated into Marseille's commercial and agricultural life.

In 1482, Provence became part of the Kingdom of France and European Jewry was persecuted. In 1492, the community was again bolstered, this time by Jews forced out of Spain during the Spanish Inquisition. A regional expulsion notice served in 1500 resulted in a wave of reluctant conversions and Jewish life effectively ended. Only in 1791 during the French Revolution were French Jews emancipated and by 1809, Napoleon had assimilated them into French life.

During the 19th century, Jews from elsewhere in France came to Marseille, where their number grew from 440 in 1808 to 2500 in 1897. During the 1930s, this number increased dramatically with refugees arriving from Nazi Germany and Eastern Europe. By 1942, around 40,000 were sheltered in Marseille, many in the neighbourhood of Le Panier (2nd). A Nazi round-up in January 1943 saw many Jews deported to the death camps (see no. 21). A lucky few, including artist Marc Chagall (1887–1985), escaped with the help of the American Emergency Rescue Committee. By the time Marseille was liberated in 1944, just 12,000 Jews remained.

Again the Jewish population recovered, this time with the arrival in 1962 of Jews from Algeria and Tunisia following decolonisation. The result today is a heterogeneous community of around 70,000 members (Europe's third largest after Paris and London), with fifty-five synagogues hosting a variety of rites. The oldest is the Great Synagogue of Marseille (Grande Synagogue de Marseille) at 117 Rue Breteuil (6th). Opened in 1864 to serve a well-to-do Sephardic community in the Opéra, Préfecture, and Vauban neighbourhoods, its Romano-Byzantine design is credited to architect Nathan Salomon (1815–1864). Set back from the road, only a plain stone

The Star of David in a window at the Great Synagogue of Marseille

Decalogue on the roof distinguishes it from a church. Inside is a different story, where in addition to the usual *Torah* cabinet *(Aron hakodesh)* and raised reading platform *(Bimah)*, there are colourful stained glass windows depicting the Star of David, twinkling crystal chandeliers, and even an organ permitted in 1856 by the country's Chief Rabbi. There is seating for 800 worshippers, with men on the ground floor and women on the balcony. The current congregation numbers approximately five thousand.

As well as the city centre community served by the Great Synagogue, there are other long-established Jewish communities in the Sainte-Marguerite (9th) and La Rose (13th) neighbourhoods, each with its own synagogue and schools. The Tiféreth Israël Synagogue in Sainte-Marguerite dates from the 1960s and takes the form of a truncated, concrete pyramid designed by Tunisian architect Fernand Boukobza (1926–2012).

Other locations nearby: 36, 38

38 The Good Mother's Basilica

It is no surprise that the Catholic Basilica of Notre-Dame de la Garde (Basilique Notre-Dame de la Garde) is Marseille's best-known symbol. Perched on top of a limestone crag and visible for miles, it is an irresistible goal for pilgrims and visitors alike (see front cover). Around two million of them visit annually, drawn by the basilica's location and the affection the Marseillais have for the building they look to for protection, hence the nickname *La Bonne Mère* (The Good Mother).

The first documented activity on La Garde hill dates back to 1218, when a local priest, one Master Pierre, erected a chapel dedicated to the Virgin Mary. In 1302, the chapel was joined by an observation post and beacon, one of a series of such installations ordered by Charles II of Anjou (1254–1309) to help protect the coast of Provence. Being the highest natural point in the city (531 feet above sea level) made La Garde the obvious location.

During the early-15th century, the chapel was replaced by a larger building. Similarly, during the early-16th century, the observation post was replaced by a fort commissioned by King Francis I (1494–1547) to help resist the 1536 siege of Marseille by Emperor Charles V (1500–1558). The hilltop chapel and

The Basilica of Notre-Dame de la Garde on its limestone crag

fort also provided a landmark for fishermen and sailors. Those who survived shipwrecks had traditionally given thanks and deposited *ex-votos* at the Church of Notre-Dame du Mont at 1 Rue de Lodi (6th). By the late-16th century, they were instead making the trek to the top of La Garde.

Closed during the Revolution, the chapel re-opened in 1807 by which time the fort had been abandoned. The chapel, however, became increasingly popular and in 1852 approval was given by the Minister of War to build a new and larger church on the disused fort's foundations. Construction began a year later and continued for the next forty years. Designed by the architect Léon Vaudoyer (1803–1872), the finished basilica consists of a church in neo-Byzantine style, with a façade of banded green Gonfolina sandstone and white Calissane limestone. Its most prominent feature is its square belfry (135 feet high) topped with a cylindrical pedestal (41 feet), which supports a huge gilded copper statue of the Madonna and Child (37 feet). Some 30,000 sheets of 23-carat gold are required for each re-gilding, which in 2024 cost 2.5 million Euros.

Inside, the basilica is richly decorated with Venetian mosaics. *Ex-voto* model ships from thankful seafarers hang from the ceiling and marine paintings adorn the walls (see frontispiece page 2). The silver Virgin on the altar pre-dates the basilica. Beneath the basilica is a rock-cut neo-Romanesque crypt, where votive candles are lit. Another statue, the Virgin of the Bouquet, also pre-dates the basilica above. Tragically, it was here that Vaudoyer's pupil, the architect Henri-Jacques Espérandieu (1829–1874), who acted as project manager, contracted the pneumonia that took him to an early grave.

After visiting the basilica museum, head back downhill either through the Bompard neighbourhood, with its narrow streets and cafés, or through Roucas Blanc to the Corniche Kennedy.

Each 15th August, pilgrims and devotees make their way up to the basilica to honour the feast of the Assumption of Mary into Heaven. From 1892 onwards, some of them would have arrived by means of a water-powered funicular railway that connected Rue Dragon (6th) with an aerial walkway that led directly to the basilica. Clearly visible in old photographs, this extraordinary construction was unfortunately demolished in 1967 after having transported 20 million passengers.

Other locations nearby: 37

39 The First Colonial Exhibition

Secteur IV (8th Arrondissement), the former site of the Marseille Colonial Exhibition (Exposition Coloniale Marseille) in Parc Chanot at the junction of Boulevard Michelet and Rond-Pont du Prado

Between April and November 1906, Marseille staged the first dedicated, state-sponsored French Colonial Exhibition (Exposition Coloniale Marseille). Its *faux* African palaces and Asian pavilions attracted 1.8 million visitors. Whilst many attended for the novelty of seeing things they had only ever imagined, others came to secure investment in the country's overseas empire and to reaffirm Marseille's position as the maritime capital of France. The latter was important given that the opening of the Suez Canal in 1869 had benefitted Marseille's northern competitors, who were also taking advantage of the arrival of steamships.

France established two colonial empires. The first consisted of colonies carved out during the 16th century in the Americas, the Caribbean, and India. By 1814, these had all been either lost or sold. The second began with the invasion of Algiers in 1830 and continued with colonies in Africa (including Morocco, Tunisia, and Madagascar), Indo China (Vietnam, Laos, and Cambodia), and the South Pacific (French Polynesia). By the time of the First World War, it was second only to the British Empire.

Only these gates survive from the 1922 Marseille Colonial Exhibition

Against this backdrop, Marseille's Colonial Exhibition was organised by influential industrialist Jules Charles-Roux (1841–1918), and Édouard Marie Heckel (1843–1916), who had founded the city's Musée Coloniale in 1893. The exhibition grounds at the junction of Boulevard Michelet and Rond-Pont du Prado (8th Arrondissement) covered 40 hectares. At their heart was a central avenue linking the main entrance with the exhibition's main building, the Grand Palais (or Palais de l'Export). Here Marseille's homegrown industries – soap, shipbuilding, olive oil, furniture, and sulphur – were promoted, with individual pavilions built for Marseille-based drinks' brands, notably Noilly Prat, Picon, and Velten. The avenue was flanked by thirty pavilions, each mimicking the architecture of a particular colony, or representing a trade that relied on colonial imports (rubber, gum, and cotton from West Africa, for example). Although Marseille was known primarily as an *entrepôt,* during the first half of the 20th century it became an industrial and manufacturing centre, too.

So successful was the exhibition that it was followed in 1922 by another. Using the same site, it again comprised a series of pavilions reflecting the architecture of the colonies. Visitors this time could walk down a street in Hanoi, visit a palace in Madagascar, and enjoy a show given by Cambodian dancers in a reconstruction of the temple at Angkor. Again, the exhibition was a success, with more than three million visits recorded.

Certainly, both exhibitions strengthened trading links between the colonies and metropolitan France. However, behind the razzmatazz, the realities of French colonialism were rather different. Proclaiming itself a civilising mission *(Mission Civilisatrice),* French colonialists viewed non-Europeans as needing re-education. The granting of French citizenship to natives was not a right but rather a privilege given only to the few. By 1936, although the colonial population had reached 69.1 million, the vast majority remained French subjects and not citizens.

After the second exhibition closed, the site was cleared. Part of it became a public park, Parc Chanot, named for Algerian-born, three-time Mayor, Jean-Baptiste Amable Chanot (1855–1920). The rest became the city's exhibition centre, which today hosts the annual Marseille International Fair. All that remained of the exhibitions was the ornate main gate on the Prado roundabout, which today forms the entrance to the park.

Like the exhibitions, eventually the colonial empire was broken up, too. The signing of the 1954 Geneva Accords saw France withdraw from its colonies in French Indochina. This was followed by Morocco (1956) and Algeria (1962), and eventually those in the South Pacific, where Vanuatu was last to gain independence in 1977.

Other locations nearby: 40, 43

40 The Vélodrome Stadium

Secteur IV (8th Arrondissement), the Orange Vélodrome Stadium (Stade Orange Vélodrom) at 3 Boulevard Michelet

One of the best sea views in Marseille is from the Pharo headland above Fort Saint Nicholas (Fort Saint-Nicolas). The scenery inland, however, is no less striking. Look to the south-east and two miles' worth of city is seemingly compressed into a much shorter distance. The focal point is the Orange Vélodrome Stadium (Stade Orange Vélodrome), Marseille's premier sporting venue, which stands out like a giant white lifebuoy.

The story of the stadium is inextricably linked with that of the Olympique de Marseille football club, which has been based there since the stadium's opening in 1937. Known simply as OM, the club began in 1892 as a general sports' club founded by René Dufaure de Montmirail, a French sports' official. It went under various names until 1899, when the club adopted the name 'Olympique' to mark the 2,500 years since the founding of Marseille by the Greeks.

Initially, rugby was the club's main sport, indeed the club's motto, *Droit au But* (Straight to the Goal) is a rugby reference. Only in 1902 did football gain prominence. Based in those days at the Huveaune Stadium (Stade de l'Huveaune), OM quickly dominated Marseille's other football teams beating them all in 1904 to win the first *Championnat du Littoral*.

Since then OM has enjoyed a long and colourful career, cheered on by its ardent fans. Despite various ups and downs, it has so far won nine league titles, ten *Coupe de France* titles, *three Coupe de la Ligue* titles, and three *Trophée des Champions* titles. It has also played in three UEFA Europa League finals, and in 1993 it became the only French club to ever win the UEFA Champions League, defeating Milan 1–0 in the final. Additionally, OM is the only French club yet to have appointed a black president, namely the Franco-Senegalese Pape Diouf (1951–2020).

The Orange Vélodrome Stadium (the 'Orange' sponsorship prefix dates from 2016) was built in 1937 on former military grounds. As its name suggests, it was originally designed as a cycle track but with facilities for other sports, too. OM first used the stadium on 13th June 1937 for a friendly match against Italy's Torino FC. The club was reluctant to relocate, however, since it owned the Huveaune Stadium. Only in 1960 did the City Council reduce the rent at the Vélodrome and the club moved there permanently.

During the 1970s, when cycle races became less common, seating was constructed over the banked track. Until it was removed permanently in the 1980s, fans of OM used the track as a slide to invade the pitch at the end of matches! Criticised for its lack of a roof, exposure to strong winds, and poor acoustics, the Vélodrome was subsequently rebuilt and by 2014 nothing remained of the original structure. Today, with its four huge stands and undulating roofline, it is the second largest stadium in France, with a capacity of 67,394 spectators.

The Orange Vélodrome Stadium dominates the 8th Arrondissement

High attendances are always guaranteed for Le Classique, when OM plays its great rival, Paris Saint-Germain. The booming soundtrack to such games is homegrown: Massilia Sound System's reggae sung in regional Provençal *(Occitan)*; Fonky Family's *Les Bad Boys de Marseille*; Soprano's *Halla Halla*, the video for which was filmed at the Vélodrome; and rap collective 13 Organisé's *En bande organisée*, with its catchphrase lyrics "C'est pas la capitale, c'est Marseille, bébé"!

The area surrounding the Vélodrome has seen much urban renewal, including the Centre Commercial du Prado Shopping Centre, the Marseille Chanot Convention and Exhibition Centre, and the Delort Stadium (Stade Delort), which hosts rugby and athletics.

Other locations nearby: 39, 41, 48

41 A Flair for Faience

Secteur IV (8th Arrondissement), the Château Borély Museum of Decorative Arts, Faience and Fashion (Musée des Arts décoratifs, de la Faïence et de la Mode) in Parc Borély at 132 Avenue Clot Bey

Today's visitors tend to associate Marseille with tourist-friendly products such as soap and *pastis*. It is all too easy to forget that the city was once a manufacturing centre for many other commodities, too, including playing cards and pottery known as faience.

A playing card factory once stood at Rue d'Aubagne 8 (1st). It was founded by master cartier Nicolas Conver (1784–1833), who is credited with having engraved the famous *Tarot de Marseille*, an Italian-suited deck used for divination. That it is dated 1760, however, suggests that Conver took a 16th century wooden printing block and simply added his own name. Invented purely as gaming cards in 1480 in Italy, the cards were imported by French soldiers and only from the late-18th century onwards were they used as a divinatory tool.

When it eventually closed in the 1970s, Conver's factory, known through marriage as Maison Camoin, was the last of Marseille's card makers. Its products are now the domain of collectors and museums,

Detail of a blue-painted faience plate by Pierre Clérissy

and the same can be said of Marseille's faience pottery. Faience is defined as earthenware coated in lead glaze to which white tin oxide has been added, creating a shiny, opaque base for painted decoration. Its invention occurred somewhere in the Middle East, probably Iraq, during the ninth century BC.

Faience arrived in Spain with the Moors in 711 AD after their conquest of the Iberian Peninsula. From there it spread to Italy during the 15th century, notably the town of Faenza whence the name Faience derives, and then Holland and France a century later. Demand was driven by the emergence of a new middle class looking for luxury products, and the adoption of more formal dining manners. During the 17th century, Rouen and Nevers were the leading French faience centres, with several secondary centres, including Marseille. The first faience factory in Marseille was founded in 1677 by Pierre Clérissy (1651–1728) in the neighbourhood of Saint-Jean-du-Désert (12th). By 1787, on the eve of the French Revolution, there were nine faience manufacturers in Marseille. The production of cheaper French porcelain and imports of English creamware, however, meant the fashion for faience was brief.

Fortunately, interest in Marseille-made faience has remained high, so much so that a dedicated museum was founded in 1995 in the Château Pastré (8th). In 2013, the collection relocated to a new location, the Château Borély at 132 Avenue Clot Bey (8th), where it forms a part of the Museum of Decorative Arts, Faience and Fashion (Musée des Arts décoratifs, de la Faïence et de la Mode). Counted among the finest faience collections in Europe, it includes works by all the great Marseille manufacturers, including Pierre Clérissy and his distinctive blue-painted plates and pharmacy jars, as well as the Oriental designs of Veuve Perrin and the delicately drawn flowers and insects of Gaspard Robert.

Completed in 1778 for the family of the wealthy merchant and shipowner Louis Borély (1692–1768), Château Borély is a fine example of a Provençal country house known as a *bastide* and retains many of its original interiors (see no. 44). It is surrounded by a landscaped public park added during the 19th century, with canals and tree-lined alleys. Adjacent is Marseille's municipal botanical garden established in 1913 by the botanist and expert in tropical medicine, Édouard Marie Heckel (1843–1916).

The Huveaune river defines the northern perimeter of Parc Borély. Beyond it is the seaside Parc Balnéaire du Prado, a curious feature of which is a monument to Arthur Rimbaud (1854–1891), the pre-Modernist poet who died young in a Marseille hospital. In the form of a disjointed shipwreck, it references Rimbaud's poem *Le Bateau Ivre* (The Drunken Boat).

Other locations nearby: 43

42 Secret of the Calanques

Secteur VI (8th Arrondissement), a trip to the Calanque des Goudes and Calanque de Callelongue in the Calanques National Park (Parc National des Calanques) (note: take bus 19 from Castellane or Rond Point du Prado to La Madrague de Montredon, then bus 20 to Port des Goudes; alternatively, during the summer months the calanques can be viewed from the sea by boat)

Marseille's 8th and 9th Arrondissements are unique in encompassing urban areas in the north and part of Europe's first peri-urban national park to the south. The Calanques National Park (Parc National des Calanques), which stretches as far east as La Ciotat, is renowned for its jagged white sea cliffs *(falaises)*, rocky coves *(calanques)*, and offshore islets *(îlots)*. With stringent regulations protecting its natural beauty and diversity, the park is a haven for walkers and nature lovers, sailors, swimmers, and divers.

It is therefore a shock to learn that until a century ago the *calanques*, especially those between Montredon and Callelongue, were hotspots for the chemical and metallurgical industries. Some twenty factories produced soda for the soap industry, lead for pipes and paint, tartaric acid for the food industry, and sand for glass, as well as sulphuric and hydrochloric acids. Indeed, so important were they to the Marseille economy that it was even suggested the Old Port extension be located here rather than in La Joliette! Fortunately, that never happened and today only a few chimneys, converted factory buildings, and still-toxic slag heaps remain to tell the story.

This tour takes in the two *calanques* that form the western gateway to the park. First is the Calanque des Goudes. Like all *calanques* it is a rocky inlet formed by a combination of river erosion and changing sea levels. A factory first appeared here in 1810, as per the terms of a Napoleonic decree to relocate polluting industries away from the city. Located at the water's edge to facilitate easy shipment, it produced soda. Later, in 1854, it was joined by a lead works built in the village itself, which remained operational until 1879. Nothing remains today leaving Goudes a picturesque village of traditional fishermen's huts *(cabanons)*, a church, grocer's shop, fish restaurants, and a population of year-round residents determined to keep things this way.

Continue now on the main road south to a track on the right-hand side. This leads across the hillside above Les Goudes towards

The Calanque de Callelongue

Cap Croisset passing a graffitied coastal gun emplacement, once part of Hitler's Mediterranean Wall *(Südwall)*. The views out to Île Maïre and its islet Tiboulen de Maïre are stunning (see back cover).

Return to the main road and continue south. Pause at the last bend before reaching Calanque de Callelongue. A scramble down rocks to the water's edge here reveals a collection of four large rusty wheels. These are the remains of the *Téléscaphe*, a novel underwater cable car built in 1966 that transported paying tourists to Goudes and back. With running costs ruinously high, however, it closed after just one year.

The road runs out at the Calanque de Callelongue. A hamlet sheltered by steep cliffs, it, too, has a forgotten industrial past. A sulphuric acid and soda factory operated here between 1849 and 1884. Unlike Goudes, however, there are several remains, including a pair of former factories (one of which is now an unexpectedly grand restaurant), a wharf, and old workers' housing clinging to the rocks above. Note, too, the old semaphore station on the hill.

By the mid-20th century, the industries of the *calanques* had either closed or else relocated to new industrial zones at Étang de Berre and Fos-sur-Mer, north of Marseille. Public opinion had changed, too, and the *calanques* were now places to be treasured and not tainted. The dozen beautiful *calanques* east of Callelongue are clear proof of this. Even the extensive ruins of a lead processing plant at the Calanque de l'Escallette farther north have been softened not only by encroaching nature but also by seasonal collections of modern art.

43 Le Corbusier's Housing Unit

Secteur IV (8th Arrondissement), the Unité d'Habitation at 280 Boulevard Michelet

Marseille is a city of high-rises. Multi-storey apartment blocks pierce the suburban skyline, some clustered into formidable estates. There are many in the Northern Districts *(Quartiers Nord)*, thrown up hurriedly during the 1960s and 70s to house immigrant workers. Plagued by unemployment and social problems, some have since been demolished. Others, notably the sprawling La Rouvière complex (1975) in the city's wealthier eastern neighbourhoods have fared much better. With its shops, banks, doctors, nursery school, and tennis court, it has been described as 'a city within a city'.

Le Corbusier's influential Unité d'Habitation

Whatever the location, Marseille's apartment blocks all owe something to one building: the Unité d'Habitation (Housing Unit) at 280 Boulevard Michelet (8th). The city's first residential tower block, it was completed in 1952 to a design by Swiss-French architect Charles-Édouard Jeanner-et-Gris (1887–1965), better known as Le Corbusier.

The Unité d'Habitation, or 'Housing Unit', represents the conclusion of the architect's quest for a guiding design principle for the construction of high-density city housing. It was based on his Modulor principle, a 1.8 metre measurement system derived from the height of a standing man with one arm stretched upwards. Le

Corbusier believed this allowed for a more comfortable relationship between humans and their living space, as opposed to that offered by the metric system. Le Corbusier sought his initial inspiration from the Narkomfin Building (1932), a Soviet communal housing project designed by modernist architect Moisei Ginzburg (1892–1946).

The Unité d'Habitation comprises 337 apartments of 14 different designs, spread across 18 levels. The whole is supported on a grid of slim, reinforced concrete pylons known as pilotis, which prevents damp and instills lightness. They are one of Le Corbusier's Five Points of Architecture, the other four being freedom from load-bearing partition walls, an unrestrained façade, ribboned windows illuminating rooms equally, and a flat roof garden providing insulation and extra space. Le Corbusier's chosen material was *béton brut* (rough-cast concrete) due to a post-war steel shortage, which spawned the Brutalist style.

Inside there are wide access corridors ('streets in the sky') running the length of the building on every third floor, with balconies at both ends. Each apartment is a duplex built across two storeys so that the room on one side of a corridor belongs to the apartment below, and the room on the opposite side belongs to the apartment above. On those floors without corridors, the apartments stretch the building's full width. Novel room features include built-in furniture and storage units, and space-saving kitchens, many of which are still used today. External decoration is minimal beyond the multi-coloured balconies. See if you can find the concrete frieze of men with raised arms, a reminder of Le Corbusier's all-important Modulor principle. The building also includes shops, a restaurant, nursery, and a hotel, which offers guests the chance to sleep in what is now a UNESCO World Heritage Site. The flat roof is designed as a multi-purpose communal terrace, with a running track, children's paddling pool, cinema, and gallery space.

The Unité d'Habitation served as a model for four other buildings by Le Corbusier, three in France and one in Berlin. Of near identical plan, all five structures, with their well-conceived proportions, ample facilities, and attractive locations, have proved popular with successive generations of occupants. They have in turn inspired other Brutalist housing complexes from Minneapolis and New Delhi to Glasgow, Warsaw, and Zagreb, including half a dozen in London, notably Ernö Goldfinger's Balfron Tower (1967) and Trellick Tower (1972). Had more been built, they might have realised Le Corbusier's dream of a modern planned metropolis radiating out from its centre, his so-called *Cité Radieuse*.

Other locations nearby: 40, 41, 44

44 The Bastides of Marseille

Secteur V (9th Arrondissement), the Bastide de la Magalone at 245 Boulevard Michelet

In 1673, the *Grande Dame* of French letter writing, Madame de Sévigné (1629–1696), visited Marseille. As she descended towards the city through the northern neighbourhood of La Viste (15th) she declared "I am charmed by the singular beauty of this city". Undoubtedly part of this beauty was the Provençal country mansions known as *bastides*.

Garden statuary at the Bastide de la Magalone

The wealthiest inhabitants of late-17th century Marseille, including powerful families and successful merchants, usually had two homes: a town house *(hôtel)* in the city and a *bastide* in the country. The *bastide* served as a place of leisure and as an agricultural estate. Away from the heat and commotion of the city, the *bastide* provided its owners with a summer getaway, where they could enjoy country pursuits, whilst their tenant farmers maintained the land.

The first *bastides* were generally five or seven-bay buildings, with a sloping, four-sided roof. They were surrounded by formal gardens to which water features were added following the arrival in 1849 of the Canal de Marseille (see no. 33). Interiors were showy, with public rooms decorated in marble and gilded stucco. During the Great Plague of 1720 and the cholera epidemic of 1835, the *bastides* of Marseille became refuges for the fortunate few.

During the 19th century, Marseille's well-to-do brought the *bastide* to the seaside in the form of glamorous villas. Three examples overlook the Corniche Kennedy (7th): the Villa Valmer (1865), which is currently being converted into a hotel; the Villa Castellamar (1884), which was later acquired by Swiss *pastis* magnate Charles Berger and is today the Promicea thalassotherapy centre; and the Villa Gaby, once home to singer and dancer Gaby Deslys (1881–1920).

It is remarkable to think that in 1807 there were around five thousand *bastides* in Marseille. Of these barely 250 remain today, with the majority lost to urban development. Few remain in private hands and instead now serve as hospitals, museums, youth hostels, and retirement homes. Typical is the large yellow Bastide de la Magalone at 245 Boulevard Michelet (9th). Built in 1690 for a wealthy Marseille merchant, its Italianate design by architect Pierre Puget (1620–1694) and surrounding formal garden by landscape designer Édouard André (1840–1911) reflect the golden age of the *bastides*. It appears especially striking today having been encroached on by modern buildings, including Le Corbusier's Unité d'Habitation apartment block (see no. 43). After passing through the hands of various owners, the building is currently occupied by the Cité de la Musique de Marseille, which opens the lovely grounds during music lessons.

A handful of other *bastides* are located in the region of the Bastide de la Magalone. They are: the pink-brick Château Pastré (1862) at 157 Avenue de Montredon (8th), where Countess Lili Pastré sheltered Jews and intellectuals during the Second World War; the Château Borély (1778) at 132 Avenue Clot Bey (8th), which now contains the Museum of Decorative Arts, Faience and Fashion (Musée des Arts décoratifs, de la Faïence et de la Mode) (see no. 41); the Château Maraljehan (1881) at 17 Travers du Conglu (8th), with its garden now largely built over and main gate marooned on a busy roundabout; the Château Valmante (1855) at 143 Traverse de la Gouffonne (9th) in which a secret meeting attended by Generals Eisenhower, Marshall, Montgomery, and Bradley was held in 1944 to discuss the liberation of Provence; and the Maison Blanche (1840) at 150 Boulevard Paul Claudel (9th), a former merchant's home and now town hall *(mairie)* for the 9th and 10th Arrondissements.

Other locations nearby: 43

45 The Cemetery of Saint Peter

Secteur V (10th Arrondissement), the Cemetery of Saint Peter (Cimetière Saint-Pierre) at 380 Rue Saint-Pierre

There is a green space in Marseille's 5th Arrondissement, shoehorned between an industrial zone and a motorway, which sprawls across 160 acres. This is the Cemetery of Saint Peter (Cimetière Saint-Pierre) on Rue Saint-Pierre, officially Marseille's longest street. Inaugurated on 30th December 1863, it is the third largest cemetery in France.

Since medieval times, the remains of Marseille's well-to-do Catholics were buried inside churches such as Notre-Dame des Accoules and Notre-Dame du Mont. Others made do with a common grave in parish cemeteries. As these places ran out of space, it was decided for reasons of sanitation to bury the dead farther away from the city centre. Accordingly, in 1820, the Cemetery of Saint Charles (Cimetière Saint-Charles) was opened on the site occupied today by Place Victor Hugo (3rd) and the Science Faculty of the Aix–Marseille University. A century earlier, it was here, outside the city walls, that victims of the Great Plague of 1720 had been buried. Responsible for the death of 100,000 inhabitants, the bubonic plague arrived in a cargo of linen carried by the merchant vessel *Grand Saint-Antoine*.

Family tombs at the Cemetery of Saint Peter

Between 1820 and 1881, the population of Marseille more than trebled to 360,099 and with it the demand for graves. It was the Cemetery of Saint Charles reaching its capacity, as well as growing opposition from home owners in the area, that prompted the opening of the Cemetery of Saint Peter. The families of those buried in the old cemetery were given free plots in the new one on condition that they arranged for the remains to be transferred. In 1876, the Cemetery of Saint Charles closed and was later cleared for redevelopment.

A special case was that of Camille Georges, the two-year-old son of a wealthy local merchant. He had been interred in 1804 in a miniature stone pyramid in the grounds of his father's mansion on Allée Emmanuel Chabrier (8th). His remains were relocated to the Cemetery of Saint Peter in 1950 leaving the pyramid empty to this day.

The layout of the Cemetery of Saint Peter was undertaken by local architect Sixte Rey (1821–1906). For inspiration he looked to the Cemetery of Père Lachaise (1804) in Paris. This provided the blueprint for the modern French cemetery, with its clearly-delineated footpaths, sombre trees, and all manner of grave designs from simple headstones to elaborate family mausolea decorated with faience floral tributes; an impressive cluster occupies a grove of pine trees alongside the crematorium. Elsewhere, there is the grave of wealthy Marseille merchant Camille Olive, who stipulated in his will that he wished to rest in a domed funerary chapel 40 feet high designed by Marseille's Chief Architect Pascal Coste (1787–1879). Different again is the grave known as *La Dernier Baiser*, which comprises a life-sized sculpture of one Ferdinand Lains cradling the head of his wife, Augustine, as he kisses her for the last time.

The cemetery's 100,000 graves include many celebrities: the beautiful French singer and dancer Gaby Deslys (1881–1920); *avant-garde* playwright Antonin Artaud (1896–1948); artist Adolphe Monticelli (1824–1886), who influenced Van Gogh; resistance fighter and local mayor Gaston Deferre (1910–1986); sculptor Antoine Sartorio (1885–1988); and the inventors of *Noilly Prat*. And let us not forget American singer Nina Simone (1933–2003) and British novelist William Somerset Maugham (1874–1965), both of whom were cremated here. The cemetery also includes specific zones for Jews and Muslims, French Foreign Legionaries, war victims, as well as executions, including Hamida Djandoubi (1949–1977), who was the last person guillotined in France.

Other locations nearby: 34

46 Marseille and the Cinema

That Marseille is a cinema city is clear. Above the road from the airport the city's name is writ large on the hillside above. Nine huge white-painted letters spell MARSEILLE in imitation of the famous HOLLYWOOD sign. It was erected in 2016 to promote a Netflix drama series called *Marseille* and has remained in place ever since.

Marseille and the cinema have always had a strong connection. In 1895, nearby La Ciotat was the setting for one of the first projected motion pictures, the Lumière brothers' 50-second *L'Arrivée d'un Train en Gare de La Ciotat*. It was screened at Marseille's Grand Hôtel du Louvre on the Canebière just two months after the world premiere in Paris. Since then, Marseille has become a popular shooting location for films and television series. Indeed, after Paris it is the second most filmed city in France thanks to its diversity of locales, homegrown directors, and 300 days of sunshine annually. In 2019 alone, 441 shoots were registered.

To the casual observer, films featuring Marseille fall into two categories: those that celebrate everyday local life and those that trade on the city's reputation for crime and corruption. Concerning the former, the name Marcel Pagnol (1895–1974) looms large. Born in Aubagne, he found fame through a trilogy of plays – *Marius* (1929), *Fanny* (1932), and *César* (1936) – set around the Old Port (Vieux Port). All were filmed, with *Marius* becoming one of the first successful French-language talkies. Pagnol himself directed *César* by which time time he had formed his own film production company.

Later Pagnol turned to the Provençal countryside. His films *Manon des Sources* and *Ugolino* (1952) focused on the machinations of peasant life in the hills above Marseille spawning the two-volume novel *L'Eau des Collines* (1963). This was filmed successfully after Pagnol's death by Claude Berri (1934–2009) as *Jean de Florette* and *Manon des Sources* (1986).

To discover more about Pagnol visit the Château de la Buzine–Maison des Cinématographies de la Méditerranée at 56 Traverse de la Buzine (11th). Pagnol purchased this lovely late-19th century country house *(bastide)* in 1941 to create a Provençal Hollywood, only to have his project scuppered by the Second World War. Today it houses a cinema, media library, café, and a small Pagnol exhibit.

The Château de la Buzine was once home to Marcel Pagnol

Marseille's criminal reputation dates back to the mid-19th century, which explains the many French and English-language crime films it has inspired: *Justin de Marseille* (1935), *À Bout de Souffle* (1960), *Le Deuxième Souffle* (1966), *Adieu l'Ami* (1968), *Borsalino* (1970), *La Scoumoune* (1972), *The Marseille Contract* (1974), *Taxi* (1998), *Un Prophète* (2009), and *BAC Nord* (2020). The granddaddy of them all is *The French Connection* (1971) starring Gene Hackman as hardened NYPD detective Jimmy 'Popeye' Doyle, who is hell-bent on bringing down a transatlantic drug operation. Although fictional, the film reflects the reality of 1970s-era Marseille, when opium poppies grown in Turkey were illegally imported into Marseille by Corsican gangs, processed into heroin, and then shipped out to the east coast of America, often with the connivance of the authorities. The industry's demise left behind it a legacy of violence and corruption that helped inspire the dystopian *Marseille Noir* genre of literature popularised by local author Jean-Claude Izzo (1945–2000), and which still colours the output of the Marseille film industry today.

The Château de la Buzine was previously owned by wealthy shipowner Victor Régis. Together with his brother Louis, he also owned the Château Régis and the Château de la Reynarde, which stand at the edge of the neighbouring Parc des Sept Collines. Today, they house a school and care centre respectively.

47 Ruins with a View

Secteur VI (11th Arrondissement), the Oppidum des Baou de Saint-Marcel at 94–96 Traverse de la Martine (note: the site is only open for guided tours with Les Amis du Vieux Saint Marcel on European Archaeology Days www.journees-archeologie.eu)

Marseille was founded as Massalia around 600 BC by Ionian Greek colonists from Phocaea, Asia Minor (modern Turkey). Local legend has taken this fact and made it into a love story between a Greek mariner, Protis, and a local princess, Gyptis, who together established a prosperous Hellenised city-state. The mariner represents the colonists; the princess represents the Segobriges, an Iron Age Celto-Ligurian tribe already present in the region.

There are considerable vestiges of the ancient Greeks in Marseille (see no. 1). Evidence for the Segobriges, however, is more shadowy. It is known that such tribes had their own kings and dynasties, quartered in fortified hilltop settlements, indeed it is possible that the name 'Segobriges' means 'people of the mighty hillfort'. Such settlements were later given the Latin name *oppidum*. To see the ruins of two such *oppida* one must travel deep into the Marseille suburbs.

The first is the Oppidum de Verduron at 29 Boulevard du Pain-de-Sucre (15th). Overlooking the northern approaches into Marseille, so

The intriguing ruins of the Oppidum des Baou de Saint-Marcel

clearly a location with strategic importance, the site consists of thirty-six single-room homes, each 12 by 12 feet square, with fireplaces, storage facilities, and single doors opening onto a street. Archaeologists have discovered amphorae, jugs, and cups suggesting the consumption of wine, and broaches *(fibulae)* used to secure clothing.

The second is a more impressive site architecturally. The Oppidum des Baou de Saint-Marcel is located around the corner from Olympique de Marseille's football training ground, close by the hilltop convent of La Serviane. Behind a set of sturdy iron gates at 94–96 Traverse de la Martine (11th), a track leads up to a steep-sided plateau (*baou* in Provençal) at an altitude of 550 feet above sea level. Overlooking the Huveaune River valley, the site was again one with strategic importance. The plateau itself covers two hectares with clear evidence for defensive walls, and dwellings with clay-bound pebble floors set closely together along narrow streets. The existence of a tower and a well demonstrates that the site was defensible and self-sustaining, with far-reaching views westwards towards the Old Port (Vieux Port).

It is thought that Greek Massalia was initially just a coastal trading post without hinterland possessions. The Segobriges held sway inland but respected the Greeks. This cordial relationship did not endure, however, and gradually the territory of the Segobriges, which once stretched from the Massif de l'Étoile, north of Marseille, down to the Mediterranean coastline, was absorbed by the Greeks. The end was violent as witnessed by the fact that occupation of the Oppidum de Verduron ended as a result of a Greek catapult assault. By contrast, the Oppidum des Baou de Saint-Marcel enjoyed an afterlife as a surveillance post to keep watch over the outskirts of Massalia. This is backed up by ceramic finds in the form of Greek imports from the 5th century BC and Italian imports from the 2nd century BC, when the site was finally abandoned.

Unfortunately, the Oppidum des Baou de Saint-Marcel is only open a few days a year (although the plateau is clearly visible from afar). Fear not, however, since there is another ruin with a view in Saint Marcel that is open all hours. The Castrum de Saint-Marcel is Marseille's only medieval castle. Located on a steep-sided crag, it is accessible by a steep track from the end of Boulevard la Forbine (11th). First constructed in the 5th century AD on the site of another *oppidum*, its most obvious feature is a sturdy circular tower added by Charles of Anjou (1226–1285), when he brought Marseille forcibly under French suzerainty.

48 Park on the Motorway

Secteur VI (12th Arrondissement), Parc Moline at 27 Boulevard Marius Richard

Marseille's 12th Arrondissement is bisected north to south by the A507, a six-lane motorway better known as the Rocade L2 (L2 Ring Road). First mooted in the early 1930s but only built between 2016 and 2018, it connects the A50 with the D4 making it possible to bypass Marseille completely. What makes the motorway remarkable is that for much of its six miles it is concealed beneath a series of public parks.

The construction of the motorway impacted several neighbourhoods: Saint-Jean-du-Désert, Saint-Julien, La Fourragère, Saint-Barnabé, and Montolivet. These former rural villages, where vines and olives were once cultivated, had latterly become tranquil havens for many city dwellers (Saint-Julien in particular, where Julius Caesar had set up camp in 49 BC during his siege of Marseille, offers superb views over Marseille). The prospect of a thundering motorway cutting through their heart rightly prompted a vociferous campaign to ensure that any damaged landscape be reinstated.

Thankfully the campaign, which lasted several decades, was successful. It was decided that for much of its length the L2 would be concealed inside a covered trench, with linear green spaces above. To see how successful this has been, visit Parc Moline, a 27-acre eco-park on Montolivet, one of the seven hills of Marseille. A mosaic of individual gardens flows river-like around a bend in the hidden motorway. There are groves of specimen trees, a butterfly and herb garden, water features, an educational farm, and an *al fresco* 'green theatre', which hosts the annual summer Musicales de la Moline festival. All are designed to promote social cohesion and to explore the benefits of 'urban countryside'.

A pre-existing feature that has been incorporated into the garden is the Château de Bois Luzy. Originally an agricultural estate established during the 17th century, it was bought in 1853 by shipowner Charles Auguste Bazin. He built the château *(bastide)* as a second home for his wife Louise ('Luzi' for short), with mosaics commissioned from the Italian mosaicists who had worked on the Basilica of Notre-Dame de la Garde (see no. 38). Thereafter, the estate passed through various hands until 1827, when it was acquired by the City of Marseille. The château served variously as a school, police rest home, and during the Second World War as a barracks for occupying German troops. Since 1947, it has been a youth hostel.

Fans of street art will want to walk to Rue Charles Kaddouz at the southern end of the park, where the motorway makes one of its brief appearances. The retaining walls here have been legally enlivened with a vast aquatic-themed fresco by the Le Havre-born artist Jace. His cartoon Mediterranean, which features his trademark *Gouzou* figures, is designed to make passing drivers think about the impact of their vehicles on the planet's deterio-

Peaceful Parc Moline hides a busy motorway

rating ecology. Whilst Jace has certainly beautified these otherwise ugly areas, there is still concern about air pollution. Under pressure from the citizen collective that got the motorway concealed in the first place, air quality monitoring stations have been installed at the tunnel exits, which activate additional ventilators in the tunnel in the event of a pollution spike.

49 Armenians in Marseille

Secteur VII (13th Arrondissement), the Armenian Quarter around Avenue de Saint-Jérôme

For centuries, the port of Marseille has attracted both merchants and exiles. The city's Armenian community ticks both these boxes having arrived as traders during the 16th century, and then again between 1915 and 1923 as refugees fleeing the Ottoman Genocide. Housed initially in disused military camps, they subsequently established communities in various neighbourhoods (see nos. 48, 53). Today there are an estimated 80,000 Armenians in Marseille. Despite this high number and their contribution to the city – including resistance fighter Missak Manouchian (1909–1944), portrait photographer Assadour Keussayan (b. 1907), and film director Robert Guédiguian (b. 1953) – most visitors remain unaware of their presence.

The place to learn more is the Armenian Apostolic Cathedral at 339 Avenue du Prado (8th). Completed in 1931, it is dedicated to the Holy Translators (Serpotz Tarkmanchatz), that is Saint Mesrop Mashtots (362–440 AD), who invented the Armenian alphabet, and his patriarch Saint Sahak I (338–439 AD). It was financed by wealthy businessman Vahan Khorassadjian (1873-1945) and is based on the famous 5th century Etchmiadzin Cathedral in Armenia. Accordingly, it has a cross-shaped plan, with a dome supported on a cylindrical drum flanked by two smaller domes. Inside there are wall paintings but no statues, which are forbidden as a warning against idolatry. Outside are commemorative busts not only of Khorassadjian but also Bishop Grigoris Balakian (1875–1934), who consecrated the building and was one of the few intellectuals to survive the Ottoman Genocide.

The Cathedral is the most grand of eight Armenian churches in Marseille. An altogether more subtle experience is to be had in the neighbourhood of Saint-Jérôme (13th Arrondissement) (the bus journey from the city centre illustrates well Marseille's shifting demographics). A couple of street names point the way, namely Boulevard Ararat, which runs off Avenue de Saint-Jérôme, and Boulevard Charles Zeytountzian, where an Armenian parish church can be found. Again dedicated to Saints Mesrop and Sahak, it was built by public subscription in 1933 to serve the families of some 450 female carpet knotters. Between 1923 and 1946, they worked for the France Orient Carpet Company (Société Tapis France Orient), which had its largest factory here.

The carpet knotters are long gone but there are still dark-eyed Armenians in Saint-Jérôme. The church is open for Mass each Sunday at

An Armenian street name in the neighbourhood of Saint-Jérôme

10am and back on Avenue de Saint-Jérôme there are several Armenian businesses, including the grocer and takeaway Chez les Cousines at number 48, its window full of Armenian and Greek delicacies. Around the corner at 8 Place Pelabon is the Association for the Research and Archiving of Armenian Memory (Association pour la Recherche et l'Archivage de la Mémoire Arménienne), one of several institutions that support the Armenian diaspora (www.webaram.com).

Despite being surrounded by modern tower blocks, Saint-Jérôme retains something of the red-roofed village it once was. Its name honouring the man who first translated the Bible into Latin dates from 1470, when Franciscans arrived in Marseille on the initiative of René Count of Provence (1409–1480), who had a hunting estate here. A later relic of the estate is the lodge at the southern end of Avenue de Saint-Jérôme, clad in cement made to look like timber *(rocaille)*. Also of interest is the former convent of the Order of the Sisters of the Visitation of Saint Mary (Ordre de la Visitation de Sainte-Marie) farther north at 20 Boulevard Madeleine Rémusat, which now contains a cooking school and a Michelin-starred restaurant, Le Jardin du Cloître.

There are several Eastern Christian faith communities in Marseille including the Melkites, Greek Byzantine Rite Catholics who arrived as traders specialised in the import-export business with the Levant and Italy. Their Church of Saint Nicholas of Myra at 19 Rue Edmond Rostand (6th) (1821) is the oldest Eastern Christian church in Europe. There are also the Chaldeans, who worship at Notre-Dame de Chaldée-Saint-Marc, and the Maronites, who use Notre-Dame-du-Liban.

Other locations nearby: 50

50 Marseille's Missing Mosques

Secteur VII (13th Arrondissement), the Mosquée des Cèdres at 31 Rue de Marathon (note: shoes must be removed before entering the prayer hall)

A small ornate pavilion stands in a garden at 584 Avenue du Prado (8th). Built in 1861, it is a salvaged fragment of a tavern that once stood in the Jardin de la Colline Pierre Puget (13th), Marseille's oldest public garden (see no. 28). For many years the pavilion's Moorish style fooled people into thinking it was a vestige of the city's first mosque. Built in 1670, this stood in the Muslim cemetery of the Galley Arsenal (Arsenal des Galères), where Ottoman slaves who worked on the king's galleys were buried (see no. 9). Unlike the pavilion, all trace of the mosque has vanished.

So to the present, and it is estimated that one fifth of Marseille's population of 1.25 million is now Muslim. They began arriving in significant numbers during the late-1950s and 1960s, when France was decolonising its African territories. Many enjoyed some sense of belonging since Marseille is surrounded by steep hills and the sea, which quickly separates immigrants not only from their homeland but also from the rest of France. How long this will continue in a city with its fair share of unemployment and social problems, in a country that is suffering increased racial disharmony, is unclear.

Initially Muslims arriving into Marseille were content to worship in simple, unofficial prayer rooms. Inevitably, however, there were growing calls for a Grand Mosque to be built. In 2007, plans were approved for one in the northern neighbourhood of Saint-Louis (15th) overlooking the harbour. The project, however, faltered due to opposition from the right-wing Rassemblement National, as well as internal squabbles over management, and a lack of funds (religious buildings in France must be privately financed). It was a considerable blow for the already deprived social housing estates of Marseille's Northern Districts *(Quartiers Nord)* (13th–16th Arrondissements). Estates such as Kalliste-Granière-Solidarité and La Castellane, which raised footballing legend Zinedine Zidane (b. 1972), have long been associated with the city's poorest immigrants, who traditionally toiled in unglamorous local industries. With urban renewal painfully slow and poverty high, criminal gangs are rife, with a proliferation of drug trafficking and squats.

In the meantime, Marseille's Muslims have settled for a couple of smaller mosques. The Mosquée des Cèdres, which opened in 2019 in

The Mosquée des Cèdres with its latticework façade

the presence of the mayor of Marseille, was the first mosque built for the Muslims of the northern neighbourhoods. Located at 31 Rue de Marathon (13th), it is the work of architect Fawzi Chaoui-Boudghéne, who opted for a non-traditional design consisting of several interlocked cubes, with no minaret. An open latticework screen *(mashrabiya)* embellished with Arabic calligraphy imparts the Islamic call to prayer.

A second mosque, the Mosquée Arrahma Busserine, stands not far away. Located at 42 Rue Cade (14th) and inaugurated in 2023, it was designed by the same architect. It, too, features a latticework screen, with the addition of a matching dome and a slender minaret. Both mosques are worth visiting for their architecture and the communities of worshippers they serve. Non-Muslims will be accorded a warm welcome, as would be expected of a city that has an association, Marseille Espérance, dedicated to maintaining dialogue between the city's various faith groups.

The protracted conflict in Algeria that delayed that nation's independence until 1962 has often overshadowed the fact that Muslim immigrants also came to Marseille from the Comoro Islands, a former French colony in the Indian Ocean. The 70,000 in Marseille form the largest Comorian community outside the Comorian capital of Moroni.

Other locations nearby: 49, 51

51 A Museum for Motorcycles

Secteur VII (13th Arrondissement), the Motorcycle Museum (Musée de la Moto) at 18 Rue Jean Marsac (formerly Traverse Saint-Paul)

One of Marseille's more specialised museums can be found on the edge of the Malpassé and Merlan neighbourhoods, far out in the 13th Arrondissment. The Motorcycle Museum (Musée de la Moto) at 18 Rue Jean Marsac (formerly Traverse Saint-Paul) is a must for anyone with an interest in the story of two-wheeled transport. It may take a while to get there using public transport but the journey is an interesting one. Those arriving by motorcycle will undoubtedly arrive more quickly!

The museum, which is housed in a converted flour mill, opened in 1989. Displayed across five floors, each floor covering a different chronological period, are some 250 machines tracing the history of the motorcycle from its late-19th century beginnings up to the present day. Most of the exhibits, some thirty of which are unique, belong to private collectors, who make their machines available long term for the benefit of an interested public.

The world's first motorcycle was the *Daimler Reitwagen*. Powered by a petrol-fuelled internal combustion engine, it was made in 1885 in Germany by Gottlieb Daimler and Wilhelm Maybach. By the turn of the century, their light, high-speed engines would revolutionise

A well-preserved Le Grimpeur motorcycle in the Motorcycle Museum

vehicular travel by land, sea, and air. The precursor of all motorcycle engines, however, is generally credited to the De Dion-Bouton Company based in Puteaux outside Paris. Their single-cylinder, four-stroke tricycle was pioneered in 1895 and became the most successful motor vehicle in Europe between 1897 and 1901. On 13th April 1902, the French racer Georges Osmont set a two-wheel speed record of 67.79 mph on a De Dion-Bouton motor tricycle.

The oldest exhibit displayed in the museum is the Swiss *Moto-sacoche* of 1904. Meaning literally 'motor bag', it features an auxiliary motor slung bag-like from the cross-bar of a standard bicycle frame, which powered the rear wheel by means of a belt. It sold rather better than the impressive but expensive race motorcycles manufactured between 1929 and 1943 by the French company Marcel Guiget. Their experimental model of 1935 was powered by an aircraft engine!

There are plenty of other star exhibits in the museum. They include a unique collection of Grand Prix racing bikes built between 1936 and 1971 by Jean and Henri Nougier, several vintage red-painted *Moto Guzzis* from 1938 and 1939, and examples of motorcycles from the French companies *Le Grimpeur, Gnome & Rhône* and *Magnat-Debon*. There is also a selection of military motorcycles used during the Second World War, and, from more recent times, an example of the prize-winning *Triumph Bonneville T120* manufactured between 1959 and 1975. The collection is filled out with all sorts of motorcycle-related material, including trade signs, posters, outfits, and badges.

The museum is a friendly place, frequented inevitably by motorcyclists and tourists but also schoolchildren and students, for whom educational programmes are organised. Additionally, the staff participates regularly at external motorcycling events both locally and nationally. In this way the museum has brought diversity and heritage to bear on Marseille's northern neighbourhoods, which are all too often ignored when it comes to visitor attractions.

Another specialist museum in the 13th Arrondissement is the Provençal Museum (Musée Provençal) at 5 Place Des Héros Château-Gombert. Founded in 1927 by Provence aficionado Jean-Baptiste Pignol, the focus here is on everyday life during the 18th and 19th centuries. All aspects are covered from costumes and furniture to religious art and nativity scenes. Special attention is drawn to harvest traditions, notably grapes and olives. The museum is rounded out with a theatre, a library dedicated to the history, culture and folklore of the region, and an active programme of related public events.

Other locations nearby: 50

52 Soap and the City

Secteur VII (14th Arrondissement), a tour of the Savonnerie Fer à Cheval at 66 Chemin de Sainte-Marthe (note: pre-booked guided tours only at www.savon-de-marseille.com; English-language tour notes available)

Along with *pastis* and *bouillabaisse*, the product most often associated with Marseille is soap. The story of its manufacture dates back some 650 years and the best is still made the old-fashioned way. Savon de Marseille is sold in gift shops across the city, the most charming of which is Le Bazar de César at 4 Montée des Accoules (2nd).

The first soap maker in Marseille is documented in 1370. Later, in 1688, King Louis XIV (1638–1715) issued an edict stipulating that authentic *Savon de Marseille* must contain at least 72 % olive oil (hence its natural green colour) and be devoid of animal fats, dyes, perfumes, and preservatives. During Louis' reign, galley slaves turned to soap making during the winter months, when the royal galleys were laid up (see no. 9).

By the early-19th century, soap making represented 45 % of manufacturing in Marseille. By 1913, annual production topped 180,000 tonnes, and by 1924 there were 122 soap companies active in the Marseille region. With the arrival of soap powder, however, the soap industry declined and today just four traditional companies remain. All are proud members of the Union des Professionnels du Savon de Marseille (UPSM).

The oldest of them is the Savonnerie Fer à Cheval at 66 Chemin de Sainte-Marthe (14th Arrondissement). Founded in 1856 in what was originally a candle factory, the company prides itself in making soap the traditional way, using only natural raw materials, and keeping the entire process in-house. During the informative guided tours, the complete soap-making process is explained.

Firstly, ten tonnes of olive oil is poured into one of nine huge tanks *(chaudrons)* located in a 19th century hall with an impressive chestnut-timbered roof. Sodium carbonate from burnt seaweed is added and the mixture heated to boiling point. The hydrolysis of the fatty oil on contact with the alkaline seaweed ash is called saponification, which leads to the formation of salts of fatty acids and glycerol. After the glycerol is removed, the remaining salts form soap. Salt water is then added causing unwanted impurities, glycerol, and excess soda to sink to the bottom of the tank. The pure soap is further boiled to complete saponification. The resulting soap paste is then dried into pellets *(bondillons)*, which are extruded and cut into bars ready for stamping with the company's lucky horseshoe trademark, and left to harden. The whole process takes seven to ten days to complete.

In the past, Marseille soap was only sold in large 5 kg (11 lb) and 20 kg (44 lb) blocks, which had to be cut into smaller pieces. Fortunately, today it comes in more manageable 300 g (11 oz) and 600 g (21 oz) squares, as well as in a 15 g (0.53 oz) guest soap

Savonnerie Fer à Cheval is Marseille's oldest soap factory

format. A 10 kg (22 lb) self-slicing block is still available to those who prefer to cut their soap by hand. As for its usage, *Savon de Marseille* serves any number of cleansing purposes from the hand washing of delicate wool and silk garments to its use as a pesticide in agriculture. It is little wonder that the Savonnerie Fer à Cheval is today protected as an Historic Monument and recognised as an Entreprise du Patrimoine Vivant (Living Heritage Company). Upon departure be sure to visit the factory shop, where bars of soap are available in a variety of sizes, together with a range of related cleaning products.

Two other traditional Marseille soap factories, Savonnerie le Sérail at 50 Boulevard Anatole de la Forge (14th) and Savonnerie du Midi at 72 Rue Augustin Roux (15th), also offer guided tours.

53 The Buddhas of Borels

Secteur VIII (15th Arrondissement), the Phap Hoa Pagoda at 3 Chemin de la Pagode off Boulevard de la Savine

Few visitors stray far from Marseille's tourist-friendly central arrondissements. This is understandable in the case of the troubled Northern Districts *(Quartiers Nords)*, with their dilapidated tower blocks and reputation for criminal activity. However, to consider the area devoid of interest would be wrong. A case in point is the Borels neighbourhood (15th), where a pair of striking pagodas bears witness to the city's Vietnamese and Cambodian communities.

Unlike many neighbourhoods in Marseille, which grew from ancient villages, Borels was originally agricultural land, its name taken from the owners of the largest farm. The nearby canal and railway witness the development of trade and industry in the area in the 19th century. During the inter-war period, Borels witnessed an influx of Armenian refugees, who built the Orthodox Church of SS. Tatéos and Parthomios at 27 Traverse de l'Église. The completion in 1947 of the Saint-Antoine A7 motorway tunnel, with reliefs depicting a boat, the

The Phap Hoa Pagoda and garden in the neighbourhood of Borels

Abbey of Saint-Victor, and the Hôtel de Ville, is a reminder that Borels by this time was the northern gateway into Marseille.

During the second half of the 20th century, the defining architecture of Borels was the residential tower block. By 1973, thirty-five of these had been hastily thrown up on the Savine Hill to house the families of immigrant workers from North Africa. They were soon joined by Vietnamese and Cambodian war refugees after the former French colonies received independence. With over 3,000 residents, the area was later branded a 'priority district' in need of urban renewal. Many of the blocks of the Cité de la Savine have since been razed and the residents relocated to new housing units in the valley below.

Although the tower blocks are gone, two Vietnamese Buddhist temples remain. Largest and most important is the Phap Hoa Pagoda at 3 Chemin de la Pagode off Boulevard de la Savine. Founded in 1978 by the *Grand Vénérable* monk Thich-Thien-Dinh, the two-storey temple building has an elaborate altar with statues of the Buddha on both floors, as well as candlelit shrines to departed members of the congregation. The temple garden contains a large reclining Buddha, a temple bell adorned with swastikas (the Sanskrit symbol of good fortune), and a gilded Buddha at the top of a flight of steps. There is also the founder's mausoleum in the form of a miniature pagoda. Even if you are not one of the city's 3,000 Buddhists, you will always be made welcome, especially on the first Sunday of the month, when worshippers gather after prayers to enjoy a vegetarian lunch.

A little way south, at 226 Chemin de Saint-Antoine-à-Saint-Joseph, is the Pho Da Pagoda. Despite being a more modest structure, this is where the Vietnamese community celebrate their New Year and other festivities. Again, there are numerous representations of the Buddha on display.

Marseille's third Buddhist temple is located at 176 Boulevard de la Forbine in the far-off 11th Arrondissement. The Truc Lâm Pagoda was established in 1970 by the Cambodian community, its location in the tranquil wooded foothills of Saint-Marcel make it the ideal venue for Tai Chi and Yoga classes, which are held every Saturday.

Let's not forget the Laotians, who together with the Vietnamese and Cambodians make up the Indochine diaspora. They had a modest 19th century trading presence in Marseille and increased dramatically following the Laotian Civil War and the Communist takeover of their homeland. They do not have their own temple in Marseille but for an idea of how one might look see old photos of the Laos Pavilion at the 1906 Marseille Colonial Exhibition (Exposition Coloniale Marseille).

54 Shipping Container Shopping

Secteur VIII (15th Arrondissement), the Marseille International Fashion (MIF68) Shopping Mall at 1 Avenue de l'Argilité

Well off the beaten tourist track, alongside a busy motorway in the northern suburbs, is something surprising. Located at 1 Avenue de l'Argilité (15th) is Marseille International Fashion (MIF68), a shopping mall made entirely from old shipping containers.

The shipping container has become something of an icon in modern times. Essentially a reuseable steel freight container, it can be moved from one mode of transport to another without unloading and reloading. Its emergence in the late-20th century dramatically reduced the cost of transporting goods and made a major contribution to the globalisation of commerce.

At the time of writing there are approximately 65 million shipping containers in circulation. Of course, they are not evenly distributed but rather mostly concentrated in areas of high trade volume, notably major ports and shipping lanes. There are an estimated 6,000 container ships at sea at any given time, with 20 million shipping containers on board. Remarkably, it is thought that between 1,300 and 2,600 containers are lost at sea annually!

The widespread availability and relative cheapness of shipping containers has seen architects deploy them as an alternative to traditional building materials. As such they have been used in housing, retail, and office projects around the world. Examples include the Cité A Docks student housing project in Le Havre, the Wenckehof container village in Amsterdam, the Smoky Park Supper Club in Asheville, North Carolina, the Leavesden Film Studios, England, and the Dordoy Bazaar in Bishkek, Kyrgyzstan.

As a busy international port, Marseille has embraced the shipping container as an architectural form. At its simplest, a single container makes for the perfect fast food outlet, several of which exist in the city. More adventurous is the Collège Jean-Claude Izzo at 2 Rue d'Hozier (2nd), where a stack of shipping containers sit neatly between a lecture hall and a silo-like structure that contains an amphitheatre. The hybrid structure is typical of the architectural experimentation current in the Euroméditerranée Zone cultural and business quarter. The college itself is named in honour of Marseille-born novelist Jean-Claude Izzo (1945–2000), who found fame in the mid-1990s with the publication of three neo-noir crime novels – *Total Chaos, Chourmo,* and *Solea*

The Marseille International Fashion Shopping Centre is made from shipping containers

– known collectively as the Marseille Trilogy.

The most ambitious shipping container project is undoubtedly Marseille International Fashion shopping mall. The brainchild of Dingguo Chen, President of the Chinese Wholesalers Association of Marseille, it was opened in 2018, as part of Chen's plan to promote co-operation between French designers and Chinese textile manufacturers. It comprises ninety-five shipping containers sourced from Adaptainer, a UK company well-versed in supplying new and used containers. The placing of the containers is the work of local architect Mathieu Cherel, who opted for several rows, with walkways in between. On top of each row are single, brightly-coloured containers set at right angles to add aesthetic interest. All together the containers host over a hundred fashion boutiques offering a vast selection of clothing to shoppers.

Adjacent to the Marseille International Fashion Shopping Centre, on the border between the 15th and 16th Arrondissements, is the Centre Commercial Grand Littoral. The largest shopping centre in the Provence-Alpes-Côte d'Azur region, with floor space in excess of a million square feet, it opened in 1996. Unfortunately, because it was built on the site of a former clay quarry, subsidence meant that part of the centre was closed until 2006, and a cinema on the site was demolished.

55 The Painters of L'Estaque

Secteur VIII (16th Arrondissement), a visit to the village of L'Estaque (note: L'Estaque can be easily reached by train and between May and September by boat from the Old Port)

For the first half of the 19th century, the artists of Marseille were influenced by the naturalism of the Barbizon School near Paris. The charge of parochialism was true to the extent that their preferred subject matter was the landscape of Provence, and they were loath to interact with artists at a national level. Their number included the pre-Impressionist Adolphe Monticelli (1824–1886), whose contemporary, the poet Victor Gelu (1806–1885), was similar in that he wrote in regional Provençal *(Occitan)*.

Marseille painting only really made an impact nationally during the early 20th century. In 1906, the city staged a Colonial Exhibition (Exposition Coloniale Marseille). Its primary goals were to attract investment in the country's burgeoning empire and to reaffirm the city's image as a great Mediterannean port (see no. 39). But it also acknowledged Marseille's emerging position as an artistic force at the centre of a distinct Southern cultural region. Accordingly, the exhibition included a display of paintings by members of the newly-emerged Marseille School

The famous light and landscape of L'Estaque

(École de Marseille). Assembled by the Provençal artist Emile Loubon (1809–1863), the works shared a mutual sensitivity to Southern light and landscape rather than any all-encompassing style.

The Colonial Exhibition also prompted the formation of various societies and salons, which flourished in tandem with a blossoming of local literature. This exposed the city to influences from beyond Provence and brought it to the attention of artists from the Parisian *avant-garde*. One of them was Paul Cézanne (1839–1906).

Born in Aix-en-Provence, Cézanne spent time during the 1860s in Paris, where he fell under the thrall of Camille Pissarro (1830–1903), one of the founding fathers of Impressionism. In 1870, he made the first of several trips to L'Estaque (16th), a pretty working-class fishing village in the north-west corner of Marseille. He stayed there with his mother in a rented house at Place François Maleterre 2, alongside the village church. By the time of his final visit in 1886, he had produced some sixty canvasses depicting the panoramic views over the village and the sea. Rendered in a post-Impressionist style that hints at abstraction, works such as *L'Estaque et le Château d'If* capture perfectly the marine light and saturated colours of the area.

Cézanne abandoned L'Estaque due to the construction of clay tile works, which he felt scarred the landscape. This, however, did not deter other artists from following him, including Georges Braque (1882–1963), Raoul Dufy (1877–1953), André Derain (1880–1954), and Albert Marquet (1875–1947). Braque visited several times between 1906 and 1910, and in 1907 painted *Le Viaduc à l'Estaque*. The work displays Cézanne's post-Impressionist reduction of landscape to geometric forms, as well as the strong non-naturalistic colours of the Fauvist painters. However, it also shows an early interest in the new Cubist style more often associated with Pablo Picasso (1881–1973). This would be fully manifested a year later in Braque's *Maisons à l'Estaque* painted in nearby Riaux. With its houses like children's building blocks, flattened perspective, and muted palette, it is considered the world's first Cubist landscape.

L'Estaque makes for an enjoyable day trip, with its beaches, waterfront cafés, photogenic railway viaducts, and marina (the name L'Estaque derives from the Provençal *Estaco* meaning 'to tie or attach' and refers to the stake to which a boat is moored). Look out for the former fishing net factory at 110 Boulevard Roger-Chieusse, the exotic Villa Palestine at 126 Plage de l'Estaque, and Jacques Cousteau's yellow submarine farther along at number 149, which can be visited by appointment (www.lescompagnonsdusaga.org). Finish at Chez Magali, a waterfront kiosk selling *Chichis Frégis* (long fried doughnuts flavoured with orange) and *Panisses* (chick pea fries).

Opening Times

Correct at time of going to press but may be subject to change.

Abbey of Saint Victor (Abbaye Saint-Victor) (7th Arrondissement), Place Saint-Victor, daily 9am–7pm (Crypt 6pm)

Ateliers Marcel Carbonel – Santons & Art de Vivre Provençal (7th Arrondissement), 47 Rue Neuve Sainte Catherine, mid-Jan–mid-Jul & Sep Wed 9am–1pm, 2–5pm; shop Mon–Fri 9am–1pm, 2–6pm & Sat 10am–1pm, 2–6pm

Basilica of Notre-Dame de la Garde (Basilique Notre-Dame de la Garde) (6th Arrondissement), Rue Fort du Sanctuaire, daily 7am–6pm

Bastide de la Magalone (9th Arrondissement), 245 Boulevard Michelet, grounds only Jun–Aug 7am–9pm, Sep–May 7am–7pm

Boulodrome Jardin du Carenage (7th Arrondissement), near 47 Quai de Rive Neuve, open daily

Cemetery of Saint Peter (Cimetière Saint-Pierre) (5th Arrondissement), 380 Rue Saint-Pierre, daily 7.30am–5.30pm

Centre de la Vieille Charité (2nd Arrondissement), 2 Rue De la Charité, Tue–Sun 9am–6pm

Château Borély Museum of Decorative Arts, Faience and Fashion (Musée des Arts décoratifs, de la Faïence et de la Mode) (8th Arrondissement), Parc Borély, 132 Avenue Clot Bey, Tue–Sun 9am–6pm

Château de la Buzine–Maison des Cinématographies de la Méditerranée (11th Arrondissement) 56 Traverse de la Buzine, Tue–Sun 10am–1pm, 2–6pm

Château d'If (7th Arrondissement), Island of If (Île d'If), Apr–Sep 10am–6pm, Oct–Mar 10am–5pm (closed Mon), closed during bad weather; see Frioul Archipelago for ferries

Chez Michel (7th Arrondissement), 6 Rue des Catalans, daily 12–1.30pm, 8–9.30pm

Cosquer Méditerranée (2nd Arrondissement), Villa Méditerranée, Promenade Robert Laffont/Esplanade du J4, daily 9.30am–7.30pm

Cristal Limiñana (5th Arrondissement), 99–101 Boulevard Jeanne d'Arc, pastis factory tours by appointment only at www.cristal-liminana.com

Deportations' Memorial (Mémorial des Deportations) (2nd Arrondissement), Avenue Vaudoyer, Tue–Sun 9am–12.30pm, 1.30–6pm

Fort Saint Nicholas (Fort Saint-Nicolas) (7th Arrondissement), 2 Boulevard Charles Livon, Fort d'Entrecasteaux Wed–Sun 12–10pm

FRAC Sud–Cité de l'Art Contemporain (2nd Arrondissement), 20 Boulevard de Dunkerque, Tue–Sat 12–7pm, Sun 2–6pm

Friche la Belle de Mai (3rd Arrondissement), 41 Rue Jobin, daily 7am–11pm

Frioul Archipelago (7th Arrondissement), ferries depart daily from Embarcadère Frioul If at 1 Quai de la Fraternité (formerly Quai des Belges) Oct–Mar 8.30am–5pm, Apr–Jun & Sep 8.30am–7pm, Jul & Aug 7.30am–10pm

Great Synagogue of Marseille (Grande Synagogue de Marseille) (6th Arrondissement), Rue Breteuil, Mon–Fri 10am–1pm

Jardin des Vestiges (1st Arrondissement), Marseille History Museum (Musée d'Histoire de Marseille), 2 Rue Henri Barbusse, Tue–Sun 9.30am–6pm

Maison Empereur (1st Arrondissement), 4 Rue des Récolettes, Mon–Sat 10am–7pm

Marseille International Fashion (MIF68) (15th Arrondissement), Shopping Centre at 1 Avenue de l'Argilité, Mon–Sat 8.30am–6.30pm

Marseille Historic Observatory (Observatoire Historique de Marseille) (4th Arrondissement), Allée Jean-Louis Pons, Wed 2–5.30pm

Mémorial de la Marseillaise (1st Arrondissement), 23-25 Rue Thubaneau, temporarily closed for renovation

Mosquée des Cèdres (13th Arrondissement), 31 Rue de Marathon, daily 8am–11pm

Motorcycle Museum (Musée de la Moto) (13th Arrondissement), 18 Rue Jean Marsac (formerly Traverse Saint-Paul), Tue–Sat 10am–5pm

Old Port Fish Market (Marché aux Poissons du Vieux Port) (1st Arrondissement), 1 Quai de la Fraternité (formerly Quai des Belges), daily 8am–1pm

Oppidum des Baou de Saint-Marcel (11th), 94–96 Traverse de la Martine, open for guided tours Les Amis du Vieux Saint Marcel on European Archaeology Days www.journees-archeologie.eu

Palais de la Bourse (1st Arrondissement), 9 La Canebière, Mon–Fri 8.30am–5pm

Palais du Pharo (7th Arrondissement), 58 Boulevard Charles Livon, palace for events only, park daily 7am–9pm

Palais Longchamps (4th Arrondissement), Boulevard Longchamp, daily 8am–6.45pm

Parc Chanot (8th Arrondissement), Boulevard Michelet/Rond-Pont du Prado, daily 7am–9pm

Parc Moline (12th Arrondissement), 27 Boulevard Marius Richard, daily 7am–7pm

Phap Hoa Pagoda (15th Arrondissement), 3 Chemin de la Pagode off Boulevard de la Savine, Mon–Fri 9am–5pm; vegetarian lunch at 12pm every first Sun of the month

Savonnerie Fer à Cheval (14th Arrondissement), 66 Chemin de Sainte-Marthe, pre-booked guided tours only at www.savon-de-marseille.com

Underwater Museum of Marseille (Musée Subaquatique de Marseille) (7th Arrondissement), Plage des Catalans, Rue des Catalans, open all hours, guided tours by appointment www.musee-subaquatique.com

Villa Santa Lucia (7th Arrondissement), 8 Montée de la Napoule, Jul & Aug Sun–Wed 8am–2pm, rest of the year guided tours for a minimum of 10 people by appointment only tel. 0622655205, villasantalucia.mh@gmail.com; tickets with cash only

Further Reading

GUIDEBOOKS

Guide Secret de Marseille et de ses Environs (Jean-Christophe Barla), West France, 2019

Marseille Le Guide Vert (Natacha Brumard), Michelin, 2022

Guide du Marseille Colonial (Alain Castan & Nora Mekmouche), Syllepse, 2022

Marseille Inner Cities Cultural Guide (David Crackanthorpe), Signal Books Ltd. 2012

Calanques (Florent Favier & Philippe Richaud), Éditions Gilletta, 2013

111 Lieux à Marseille à ne pas Manquer, (Dominique Milherou), Emons Verlag, 2023

Marseille Insolite et Secrète (Éléonore Quemener & Jean-Pierre Cassely), Editions Jonglez, 2019

Footprint Focus Marseille & Western Provence (Tristan Rutherford & Kathryn Tomasetti), FootprintHandbooks, 2012

Marseille Insolite: Les Trésors Cachés de la Cité Phocéene (François Thomazeau), Les Beaux Jours, 2015

Le Guide du Promeneur de Marseille (François Thomazeau), Les Beaux Jours, 2018

Marseille Pocket Guide (Kathryn Tomasetti & Delphine Dewulf), Thomas Cook Publishing, 2009

A Week Abroad: Marseille (Various), Week Abroad, 2022

Marseille et les Calanques (Various), Lonely Planet, 2023

Wallpaper City Guide Marseille (Various), Phaidon, 2015

HISTORY

Une histoire de Marseille en 90 lieux: 16e-20e siècle (Judith Aziza), Editions Gaussen, 2019

Une histoire de Marseille en 90 autres lieux: 16e-20e siècle (Judith Aziza), Editions Gaussen, 2021

Dictionnaire Historique des Rues de Marseille (Adrien Blès), Jean Laffite, 2003

Histoire de Marseille (Raoul Busquet), Éditions Laffitte, 1999

Les Calanques Industrielles de Marseille et leurs Pollutions (Xavier Daumalin), Ref.2c Eds, 2016

La Grotte Cosquer en Questions: Le Paléolithique en Provence (Xavier Delestre), Éditions Equinoxe, 2021

Histoire Universelle de Marseille: De l'an mil à l'an deux mille (Alèssi Dell'Umbria), Agone, 2006

Marseille Mix (William Firebrace), Architectural Association, 2010

A Considerable Town (M. F. K. Fisher), Alfred Knopf, 1978

Crossroads Marseille, 1940 (Mary Jayne Gold), Doubleday, 1980

Wicked City: The Many Cultures of Marseille (Nicholas Hewitt), C. Hurst & Co. Publishers, 201

Histoire de Marseille en Treize Événements (Philippe Joutard), Jeanne Laffitte, 1988

Histoire de Marseille de la Révolution à nos jours (Emile Thémime), Perrin, 1999

Marseille, une Biographie (François Thomazeau), Stock, 2013

February 1933: The Winter of Literature (Uwe Wittstock), Polity, 2023

ART & ARCHITECTURE

Marseille: Une Autre Façon de Voir la Vie à Travers son Urbanisme, (Gérard Planchenault & Marcel Bajard), Editions Picard, 2022

Le Patrimoine de Marseille: Une Ville et ses Monuments (Régis Bertrand & Gilles Martin-Raget), *Éditions Jeanne Laffitte*, 2001

Mediterranean Crossroads: Marseille and Modern Architecture (Sheila Crane), University of Minnesota Press, 2011

Marseille Monuments (Catherine D'Ortoli & Catherine Dureuil-Bourachau), Parentheses, 2019

Guide du Street Art Marseille (LLB), Alternatives, 2020

The Painters of Marseille (Alfred & Betty Rozelaar-Green), Jean Laffitte, 1990

Le Corbusier: L'Unité d'habitation de Marseille/The Unité d'Habitation in Marseilles (Jacques Sbriglio), Birkhäuser, 2004

LITERATURE & TRAVEL WRITING

Le Parler Marseillais (Robert Bouvier), Jeanne Laffitte, 1985

The Count of Monte Cristo (Alexandre Dumas), Wordsworth Editions, 1997

Total Khéops, Chourmo, Solea (Jean-Claude Izzo), France Loisirs, 2001

Marseille, Porte du Sud (Albert Londres), Les Editions de France, 1927

Banjo (Claude McKay), Harper & Brothers, 1929

Romance in Marseille (Claude McKay), Penguin Classics, 2020

Transit (Anna Seghers), Aufbau-Verlag GmbH, 2013

FOOD & DRINK

Taste the World in Marseille: Marseille Cuisine by the Marseillais (Vérane Frédiani), La Martinière/Abrams, 2023

Made in Marseille: Food and Flavors from France's' Mediterranean Seaport (Daniel Young), Harper Collins, 2002

ILLUSTRATED BOOKS

Marseille, Un Siècle d'Images/A Century of Pictures (Fernand Albert), Parentheses, 2000

Marseille de nos pères (Silvie Aries & Jean Ribiere), Rouergue, 2014

Marseille: Un Ville d'Exceptions (Patrick Guzick), Equinoxe, 2013

Marseille Nouveau Portrait (Rémy Kerténian & Camille Moirenc), Jeanne Laffitte, 2013

Marseille (Joan Liftin), Damiani, 2016

WEBSITES

www.marseillesecrete.com

www.tourisme-marseille.com

www.marseille-tourisme.com

www.marseilletourisme.fr

www.madeinmarseille.net

www.marseille.ca/maps/arrondissement.html

Acknowledgements

For kind permission to take photographs, as well as for arranging access and the provision of information, the following people are most gratefully acknowledged:

Philip Adsetts, Olivier Andraud, François-Louis Athénas (Galerie des Augustins), Chris Beck, Malik Benghezal (Callelongue), Jonathan Bregliano (Les Amis du Vieux Saint Marcel), Philippa Chapman, Lydia Chiesi, Eric Fourneval (L'Estaque), Great Synagogue of Marseille (Grande Synagogue de Marseille), Father Christophe Héry (Chapelle du Bon-Jésus), Karen Jagiellowicz, Lucy Jones, Daniel Kennedy, La Maison du Pastis, Grégory Laborde (Librairie Jeanne Laffitte), Antony Lacanaud (Musée Subaquatique de Marseille), Maheva Lebreton & Hamabelle Rocha (Atelier Marcel Carbonel), Dave Part, Isabelle Racamier, Elise Renard (Villa Santa Lucia), Angela Ricca (Citadelle de Marseille), Christel Ruiz (Musée d'Histoire de Marseille), Lionel Ruiz (Andromede–Observatoire Historique de Marseille), Savonnerie Fer à Cheval, Sophie Spagnolo & Assia Salhi (Grotte Cosquer), Tony Spawforth, Biksuni Thich Giac Tu (Phap Hoa Pagoda), and Maristella Vasserot (Cristal Limiñana,). Thanks also to my brother Adrian for inspiring me to explore Marseille, my mother Mary and great cousin James Dickinson for bringing interesting news items to my attention, John Carchrae for his invaluable help in proof-reading the text, Simon Laffoley for his photo editing skills, and Digital Bits for managing my website.

Finally, heartfelt thanks to my wife, Roswitha, for her tireless support of my work and wonderful company on field trips, and to my late father, Trevor, for inspiring me to track down things unique, hidden and unusual in the first place. To you both I am beyond grateful.

Mosaic street art by Invader (see no. 35)

Imprint

1st Edition published by The Urban Explorer, 2025
A division of Duncan J. D. Smith
contact@duncanjdsmith.com
www.onlyinguides.com
www.duncanjdsmith.com

Original graphic design: Stefan Fuhrer
Typesetting and picture editing: Luke Griffin/Griffix Design
Map: www.scalablemaps.com
Printed and bound in Dubai by Oriental Press

ISBN 978-3-9505392-5-7